KU-270-842

THE CAMBRIDGE POCKET SHAKESPEARE

General Editor: JOHN DOVER WILSON

RICHARD III

RICHARD III

EDITED BY

JOHN DOVER WILSON

CAMBRIDGE

At the University Press

1959

PUBLISHED BY
THE SYNDICS OF THE CAMBRIDGE UNIVERSITY PRESS
Bentley House, 200 Euston Road, London, N.W. 1
American Branch: 32 East 57th Street, New York 22, N.Y.

First edition (The New Shakespeare) 1954
This edition (giving the New Shakespeare text and glossary with corrections) 1959

Printed in Great Britain at the University Press, Cambridge
(Brooke Crutchley, University Printer)

SHAKESPEARE'S PLAYS

This list suggests the order in which most scholars now think the plays were written, and gives approximate dates of composition. Only in a few cases is the issue beyond doubt.

Henry VI, Part I, 1589–90
Henry VI, Parts II and III, 1590–91
Richard III, 1592–93
The Comedy of Errors, 1592–93
Titus Andronicus, 1593–94
The Taming of the Shrew, 1593–94
The Two Gentlemen of Verona, 1594–95
Love's Labour's Lost, 1594–95
Romeo and Juliet, 1595–96
Richard II, 1595–96
A Midsummer Night's Dream, 1595–96
King John, 1596–97
The Merchant of Venice, 1596–97
Henry IV, Parts I and II, 1597–98
Much Ado About Nothing, 1598–99
Henry V, 1598–99
Julius Caesar, 1599–1600
The Merry Wives of Windsor, 1597–1601
As You Like It, 1599–1600
Twelfth Night, 1599–1602
Hamlet, 1600–01
Troilus and Cressida, 1601–02
All's Well that Ends Well, 1602–04
Measure for Measure, 1603–04
Othello, 1603–04
King Lear, 1605–06
Macbeth, 1605–06
Timon of Athens, 1605–08
Antony and Cleopatra, 1606–07
Coriolanus, 1607–08
Pericles, 1608–09
Cymbeline, 1609–10
The Winter's Tale, 1610–11
The Tempest, 1611–12
Henry VIII, 1612–13

An obelisk (†) implies corruption or emendation, a single bracket an aside; single inverted commas are editorial, and mark original stage directions. In plays for which Folio and Quarto texts exist, passages taken from the text not mainly used are enclosed within square brackets. Four dots normally represent a full-stop in the original. Long-armed brackets denote passages either probably not by Shakespeare or later rejected by him.

The scene: London and elsewhere in England

CHARACTERS IN THE PLAY

*KING EDWARD *the Fourth*

*EDWARD, PRINCE OF WALES, *afterwards King Edward V* } *sons to the King*
*RICHARD, *Duke of York* }

*GEORGE, *Duke of Clarence* } *brothers to King Edward*
*RICHARD, *Duke of Gloucester, afterwards King Richard III* }

**A young son of Clarence* [EDWARD PLANTAGENET]

*HENRY, *Earl of Richmond, afterwards King Henry VII*

*CARDINAL [*Thomas Bourchier, Archbishop of Canterbury*]

ARCHBISHOP OF YORK [Thomas Rotheram]

BISHOP OF ELY [John Morton]

*DUKE OF BUCKINGHAM

DUKE OF NORFOLK

EARL OF SURREY, *his son*

*ANTHONY WOODEVILLE, EARL RIVERS, *brother to Elizabeth*

*MARQUIS OF DORSET *and* *LORD GREY, *sons to Elizabeth*

EARL OF OXFORD

LORD HASTINGS

*LORD STANLEY, EARL OF DERBY

LORD LOVEL

SIR THOMAS VAUGHAN

SIR RICHARD RATCLIFFE

SIR WILLIAM CATESBY

SIR JAMES TYRREL

SIR JAMES BLOUNT

SIR WALTER HERBERT

SIR ROBERT BRAKENBURY, *Lieutenant of the Tower*

SIR WILLIAM BRANDON

CHRISTOPHER URSWICK, *a priest*
Another Priest
TRESSEL *and* BERKELEY, *gentlemen attending on the Lady Anne*
Lord Mayor of London
Sheriff of Wiltshire

*ELIZABETH, *queen to King Edward IV*
*MARGARET, *widow of King Henry VI*
*DUCHESS OF YORK, *mother to King Edward IV*
*LADY ANNE, *widow of Edward Prince of Wales, the son of King Henry VI; afterwards married to Richard*
**A young daughter of Clarence* [MARGARET PLANTAGENET]

Ghosts of those murdered by Richard III, Lords and other Attendants; a Pursuivant, Scrivener, Citizens, Murderers, Messengers, Soldiers, etc.

For the characters starred see the Genealogical Table at the end of the book.

'THE TRAGEDY OF

RICHARD THE THIRD

with the landing of Earl Richmond and the Battle at Bosworth Field'

[I. I.] *London. A street*

'Enter RICHARD, DUKE OF GLOUCESTER, *solus'*

Gloucester. Now is the winter of our discontent
Made glorious summer by this sun of York;
And all the clouds that loured upon our house
In the deep bosom of the ocean buried.
Now are our brows bound with victorious wreaths;
Our bruiséd arms hung up for monuments;
Our stern alarums changed to merry meetings;
Our dreadful marches to delightful measures.
Grim-visaged war hath smoothed his wrinkléd front;
And now, instead of mounting barbéd steeds
To fright the souls of fearful adversaries,
He capers nimbly in a lady's chamber
To the lascivious pleasing of a lute.
But I, that am not shaped for sportive tricks,
Nor made to court an amorous looking-glass;
I, that am rudely stamped, and want love's majesty
To strut before a wanton ambling nymph;
I, that am curtailed of this fair proportion,
Cheated of feature by dissembling Nature,
Deformed, unfinished, sent before my time
Into this breathing world, scarce half made up,
And that so lamely and unfashionable
That dogs bark at me as I halt by them;

Why, I, in this weak piping time of peace,
Have no delight to pass away the time,
Unless to spy my shadow in the sun
And descant on mine own deformity:
And therefore, since I cannot prove a lover,
To entertain these fair well-spoken days,
I am determinéd to prove a villain
And hate the idle pleasures of these days.
Plots have I laid, inductions dangerous,
By drunken prophecies, libels and dreams,
To set my brother Clarence and the king
In deadly hate the one against the other:
And if King Edward be as true and just
As I am subtle, false and treacherous,
This day should Clarence closely be mewed up,
About a prophecy, which says that G
Of Edward's heirs the murderer shall be.
Dive, thoughts, down to my soul—here Clarence comes.

Enter CLARENCE, *guarded, and* BRAKENBURY, *Lieutenant of the Tower*

Brother, good day: what means this arméd guard
That waits upon your grace?
Clarence. His majesty,
Tend'ring my person's safety, hath appointed
This conduct to convey me to the Tower.
Gloucester. Upon what cause?
Clarence. Because my name is George.
Gloucester. Alack, my lord, that fault is none of yours;
He should, for that, commit your godfathers:
Belike his majesty hath some intent
That you should be new-christ'ned in the Tower.
But what's the matter, Clarence? may I know?
Clarence. Yea, Richard, when I know; for I protest

As yet I do not: but, as I can learn,
He hearkens after prophecies and dreams;
And from the cross-row plucks the letter G,
And says a wizard told him that by G
His issue disinherited should be;
And, for my name of George begins with G,
It follows in his thought that I am he.
These, as I learn, and such like toys as these
Hath moved his highness to commit me now.
Gloucester. Why, this it is, when men are ruled by women:
'Tis not the king that sends you to the Tower;
My Lady Grey his wife, Clarence, 'tis she
That tempers him to this extremity.
Was it not she, and that good man of worship,
Anthony Woodeville, her brother there,
That made him send Lord Hastings to the Tower,
From whence this present day he is delivered?
We are not safe, Clarence, we are not safe.
Clarence. By heaven, I think there's no man is secure
But the queen's kindred, and night-walking heralds
That trudge betwixt the king and Mistress Shore.
Heard you not what an humble suppliant
Lord Hastings was for his delivery?
Gloucester. Humbly complaining to her deity
Got my Lord Chamberlain his liberty.
I'll tell you what, I think it is our way
If we will keep in favour with the king,
To be her men and wear her livery.
The jealous o'erworn widow and herself,
Since that our brother dubbed them gentlewomen,
Are mighty gossips in our monarchy.
Brakenbury. Beseech your graces both to pardon me;
His majesty hath straitly given in charge

That no man shall have private conference
(Of what degree soever) with his brother.
Gloucester. Even so; an't please your worship, Brakenbury,
You may partake of any thing we say:
We speak no treason, man: we say the king
Is wise and virtuous, and his noble queen
Well struck in years, fair, and not jealious;
We say that Shore's wife hath a pretty foot,
A cherry lip, a bonny eye, a passing pleasing tongue;
And that the queen's kin are made gentle-folks:
How say you, sir? can you deny all this?
Brakenbury. With this, my lord, myself have nought to do.
Gloucester. Naught to do with Mistress Shore! I tell thee fellow,
He that doth naught with her (excepting one)
Were best to do it secretly, alone.
Brakenbury. What one, my lord?
Gloucester. Her husband, knave: wouldst thou betray me?
Brakenbury. I do beseech your grace to pardon me:
Forbear your conference with the noble duke.
Clarence. We know thy charge, Brakenbury, and will obey.
Gloucester. We are the queen's abjects, and must obey.
Brother, farewell: I will unto the king;
And whatsoe'er you will employ me in,
Were it to call King Edward's widow sister,
I will perform it to enfranchise you.
Meantime, this deep disgrace in brotherhood
Touches me nearer than you can imagine.
Clarence. I know it pleaseth neither of us well.

Gloucester. Well, your imprisonment shall not be long;
I will deliver you, or else lie for you:
Meantime, have patience.
Clarence. I must perforce. Farewell.
[*Clarence, Brakenbury, and the Guard pass on*
Gloucester. Go, tread the path that thou shalt ne'er return:
Simple, plain Clarence, I do love thee so,
That I will shortly send thy soul to heaven,
If heaven will take the present at our hands.
But who comes here? the new-deliveréd Hastings?

'*Enter* LORD HASTINGS'

Hastings. Good time of day unto my gracious lord!
Gloucester. As much unto my good Lord Chamberlain!
Well are you welcome to the open air.
How hath your lordship brooked imprisonment?
Hastings. With patience, noble lord, as prisoners must:
But I shall live, my lord, to give them thanks
That were the cause of my imprisonment.
Gloucester. No doubt, no doubt; and so shall Clarence too;
For they that were your enemies are his,
And have prevailed as much on him as you.
Hastings. More pity that the eagles should be mewed,
Whiles kites and buzzards prey at liberty.
Gloucester. What news abroad?
Hastings. No news so bad abroad as this at home:
The king is sickly, weak, and melancholy,
And his physicians fear him mightily.

Gloucester. Now, by Saint John, that news is bad indeed.
O, he hath kept an evil diet long,
And overmuch consumed his royal person:
'Tis very grievous to be thought upon.
Where is he, in his bed?
Hastings. He is.
Gloucester. Go you before, and I will follow you.
[*Hastings departs*
He cannot live, I hope; and must not die
Till George be packed with post-horse up to heaven.
I'll in, to urge his hatred more to Clarence
With lies well steeled with weighty arguments;
And, if I fail not in my deep intent,
Clarence hath not another day to live:
Which done, God take King Edward to his mercy,
And leave the world for me to bustle in!
For then I'll marry Warwick's youngest daughter.
What though I killed her husband and her father?
The readiest way to make the wench amends
Is to become her husband and her father:
The which will I; not all so much for love
As for another secret close intent
By marrying her which I must reach unto.
But yet I run before my horse to market:
Clarence still breathes; Edward still lives and reigns:
When they are gone, then must I count my gains.
[*he goes*

[1. 2.] '*Enter the corpse of* HENRY *the Sixth, with halberds to guard it;* LADY ANNE *being the mourner*', *attended by Tressel and Berkeley*

Anne. Set down, set down your honourable load—
If honour may be shrouded in a hearse—

Whilst I awhile obsequiously lament
Th'untimely fall of virtuous Lancaster.
Poor key-cold figure of a holy king!
Pale ashes of the house of Lancaster!
Thou bloodless remnant of that royal blood!
Be it lawful that I invocate thy ghost,
To hear the lamentations of poor Anne,
Wife to thy Edward, to thy slaught'red son,
Stabbed by the selfsame hand that made these wounds!
Lo, in these windows that let forth thy life
I pour the helpless balm of my poor eyes.
O curséd be the hand that made these holes!
Curséd the blood that let this blood from hence!
Curséd the heart that had the heart to do it!
More direful hap betide that hated wretch
That makes us wretched by the death of thee
Than I can wish to wolves—to spiders, toads,
Or any creeping venomed thing that lives!
If ever he have child, abortive be it,
Prodigious, and untimely brought to light,
Whose ugly and unnatural aspect
May fright the hopeful mother at the view;
And that be heir to his unhappiness!
If ever he have wife, let her be made
More miserable by the life of him
Than I am by my young lord's death and thee!
Come, now towards Chertsey with your holy load,
Taken from Paul's to be interréd there;
And still, as you are weary of this weight,
Rest you, whiles I lament King Henry's corse.

'Enter RICHARD, DUKE OF GLOUCESTER*'*

Gloucester. Stay, you that bear the corse, and set it down.

Anne. What black magician conjures up this fiend,
To stop devoted charitable deeds?
Gloucester. Villains, set down the corse; or, by Saint Paul,
I'll make a corse of him that disobeys.
Halberdier. My lord, stand back, and let the coffin pass.
Gloucester. Unmannered dog! stand thou, when I command:
Advance thy halberd higher than my breast,
Or, by Saint Paul, I'll strike thee to my foot,
And spurn upon thee, beggar, for thy boldness.
Anne. What, do you tremble? are you all afraid?
Alas, I blame you not, for you are mortal,
And mortal eyes cannot endure the devil.
Avaunt, thou dreadful minister of hell!
Thou hadst but power over his mortal body,
His soul thou canst not have; therefore, be gone.
Gloucester. Sweet saint, for charity, be not so curst.
Anne. Foul devil, for God's sake, hence, and trouble us not,
For thou hast made the happy earth thy hell,
Filled it with cursing cries and deep exclaims.
If thou delight to view thy heinous deeds,
Behold this pattern of thy butcheries.
O, gentlemen, see, see! dead Henry's wounds
Open their congealed mouths and bleed afresh.
Blush, blush, thou lump of foul deformity;
For 'tis thy presence that exhales this blood
From cold and empty veins, where no blood dwells;
Thy deeds, inhuman and unnatural,
Provokes this deluge most unnatural.
O God, which this blood mad'st, revenge his death!
O earth, which this blood drink'st, revenge his death!

Either, heaven, with lightning strike the murd'rer dead,
Or earth, gape open wide and eat him quick,
As thou dost swallow up this good king's blood,
Which his hell-governed arm hath butcheréd!
Gloucester. Lady, you know no rules of charity,
Which renders good for bad, blessings for curses.
Anne. Villain, thou know'st no law of God nor man.
No beast so fierce but knows some touch of pity.
Gloucester. But I know none, and therefore am no beast.
Anne. O wonderful, when devils tell the truth!
Gloucester. More wonderful, when angels are so angry.
Vouchsafe, divine perfection of a woman,
Of these supposéd crimes, to give me leave,
By circumstance, but to acquit myself.
Anne. Vouchsafe, diffused infection of a man,
Of these known evils, but to give me leave,
By circumstance, to accuse thy curséd self.
Gloucester. Fairer than tongue can name thee, let me have
Some patient leisure to excuse myself.
Anne. Fouler than heart can think thee, thou canst make
No excuse current but to hang thyself.
Gloucester. By such despair, I should accuse myself.
Anne. And, by despairing, shalt thou stand excused
For doing worthy vengeance on thyself
That didst unworthy slaughter upon others.
Gloucester. Say that I slew them not?
Anne. Then say they were not slain:
But dead they are, and, devilish slave, by thee.
Gloucester. I did not kill your husband.
Anne. Why, then he is alive.

Gloucester. Nay, he is dead; and slain by Edward's hands.
Anne. In thy foul throat thou liest: Queen Margaret saw
Thy murd'rous falchion smoking in his blood;
The which thou once didst bend against her breast,
But that thy brothers beat aside the point.
Gloucester. I was provokéd by her sland'rous tongue,
That laid their guilt upon my guiltless shoulders.
Anne. Thou wast provokéd by thy bloody mind,
That never dream'st on aught but butcheries:
Didst thou not kill this king?
Gloucester. I grant ye.
Anne. Dost grant me, hedgehog? then, God grant me too
Thou mayst be damnéd for that wicked deed!
O, he was gentle, mild, and virtuous!
Gloucester. The better for the King of heaven, that hath him.
Anne. He is in heaven, where thou shalt never come.
Gloucester. Let him thank me, that holp to send him thither;
For he was fitter for that place than earth.
Anne. And thou unfit for any place but hell.
Gloucester. Yes, one place else, if you will hear me name it.
Anne. Some dungeon.
Gloucester. Your bed-chamber.
Anne. Ill rest betide the chamber where thou liest!
Gloucester. So will it, madam, till I lie with you.
Anne. I hope so.
Gloucester. I know so. But, gentle Lady Anne,
To leave this keen encounter of our wits,
And fall something into a slower method,

Is not the causer of the timeless deaths
Of these Plantagenets, Henry and Edward,
As blameful as the executioner?
Anne. Thou wast the cause of that accursed effect.
Gloucester. Your beauty was the cause of that effect;
Your beauty, that did haunt me in my sleep
To undertake the death of all the world,
So I might live one hour in your sweet bosom.
Anne. If I thought that, I tell thee, homicide,
These nails should rend that beauty from my cheeks.
Gloucester. These eyes could not endure that beauty's wrack;
You should not blemish it, if I stood by:
As all the world is cheerèd by the sun,
So I by that; it is my day, my life.
Anne. Black night o'ershade thy day, and death thy life!
Gloucester. Curse not thyself, fair creature; thou art both.
Anne. I would I were, to be revenged on thee.
Gloucester. It is a quarrel most unnatural,
To be revenged on him that loveth thee.
Anne. It is a quarrel just and reasonable,
To be revenged on him that killed my husband.
Gloucester. He that bereft thee, lady, of thy husband,
Did it to help thee to a better husband.
Anne. His better doth not breathe upon the earth.
Gloucester. He lives that loves thee better than he could.
Anne. Name him.
Gloucester. Plantagenet.
Anne. Why, that was he.

Gloucester. The selfsame name, but one of better nature.
Anne. Where is he?
Gloucester. Here. [*she 'spits at him'*] Why dost thou spit at me?
Anne. Would it were mortal poison, for thy sake!
Gloucester. Never came poison from so sweet a place.
Anne. Never hung poison on a fouler toad.
Out of my sight! thou dost infect mine eyes.
Gloucester. Thine eyes, sweet lady, have infected mine.
Anne. Would they were basilisks to strike thee dead!
Gloucester. I would they were, that I might die at once;
For now they kill me with a living death.
Those eyes of thine from mine have drawn salt tears,
Shamed their aspects with store of childish drops:
These eyes, which never shed remorseful tear,
No, when my father York and Edward wept,
To hear the piteous moan that Rutland made
When black-faced Clifford shook his sword at him;
Nor when thy warlike father, like a child,
Told the sad story of my father's death,
And twenty times made pause to sob and weep
That all the standers-by had wet their cheeks
Like trees bedashed with rain—in that sad time
My manly eyes did scorn an humble tear;
And what these sorrows could not thence exhale
Thy beauty hath, and made them blind with weeping.
I never sued to friend nor enemy;
My tongue could never learn sweet smoothing word;
But, now thy beauty is proposed my fee,
My proud heart sues, and prompts my tongue to speak.
['*she looks scornfully at him*'
Teach not thy lip such scorn, for it was made

For kissing, lady, not for such contempt.
If thy revengeful heart cannot forgive,
Lo, here I lend thee this sharp-pointed sword;
Which if thou please to hide in this true breast,
And let the soul forth that adoreth thee,
I lay it naked to the deadly stroke,
And humbly beg the death upon my knee.
['*he lays his breast open: she offers at it with his sword*'
Nay, do not pause; for I did kill King Henry,
But 'twas thy beauty that provokéd me.
Nay, now dispatch; 'twas I that stabbed young Edward,
But 'twas thy heavenly face that set me on.
['*she falls the sword*'
Take up the sword again, or take up me.
Anne. Arise, dissembler: though I wish thy death,
I will not be thy executioner.
Gloucester. Then bid me kill myself, and I will do it.
Anne. I have already.
Gloucester. That was in thy rage:
Speak it again, and even with the word
This hand, which, for thy love, did kill thy love,
Shall, for thy love, kill a far truer love;
To both their deaths shalt thou be accessary.
Anne. I would I knew thy heart.
Gloucester. 'Tis figured in my tongue.
Anne. I fear me both are false.
Gloucester. Then never was man true.
Anne. Well, well, put up your sword.
Gloucester. Say, then, my peace is made.
Anne. That shalt thou know hereafter.
Gloucester. But shall I live in hope?
Anne. All men, I hope, live so.
Gloucester. Vouchsafe to wear this ring.
Anne. To take is not to give. [*she puts on the ring*

Gloucester. Look how my ring encompasseth
thy finger,
Even so thy breast encloseth my poor heart;
Wear both of them, for both of them are thine.
And if thy poor devoted servant may
But beg one favour at thy gracious hand,
Thou dost confirm his happiness for ever.
Anne. What is it?
Gloucester. That it may please you leave these
sad designs
To him that hath most cause to be a mourner,
And presently repair to Crosby House;
Where, after I have solemnly interred
At Chertsey monast'ry this noble king,
And wet his grave with my repentant tears,
I will with all expedient duty see you:
For divers unknown reasons, I beseech you,
Grant me this boon.
Anne. With all my heart; and much it joys me too,
To see you are become so penitent.
Tressel and Berkeley, go along with me.
Gloucester. Bid me farewell.
Anne. 'Tis more than you deserve;
But since you teach me how to flatter you,
Imagine I have said farewell already.
[*she goes, followed by two of the halberds*
Gloucester. Sirs, take up the corse.
Halberdier. Towards Chertsey, noble lord?
Gloucester. No, to Whitefriars; there attend
my coming.
[*they carry away the corpse*
Was ever woman in this humour wooed?
Was ever woman in this humour won?
I'll have her; but I will not keep her long.

What! I, that killed her husband and his father,
To take her in her heart's extremest hate,
With curses in her mouth, tears in her eyes,
The bleeding witness of my hatred by;
Having God, her conscience, and these bars against me,
And I no friends to back my suit at all,
But the plain devil and dissembling looks,
And yet to win her! all the world to nothing!
Ha?
Hath she forgot already that brave prince,
Edward, her lord, whom I, some three months since,
Stabbed in my angry mood at Tewkesbury?
A sweeter and a lovelier gentleman—
Framed in the prodigality of nature,
Young, valiant, wise, and, no doubt, right royal—
The spacious world cannot again afford:
And will she yet abase her eyes on me,
That cropped the golden prime of this sweet prince,
And made her widow to a woeful bed?
On me, whose all not equals Edward's moiety?
On me, that halts and am misshapen thus?
My dukedom to a beggarly denier,
I do mistake my person all this while:
Upon my life, she finds, although I cannot,
Myself to be a marv'llous proper man.
I'll be at charges for a looking-glass,
And entertain a score or two of tailors,
To study fashions to adorn my body:
Since I am crept in favour with myself,
I will maintain it with some little cost.
But first I'll turn yon fellow in his grave;
And then return lamenting to my love.
Shine out, fair sun, till I have bought a glass,
That I may see my shadow as I pass. [*he goes*

[1. 3.] *London. The palace*

'Enter the QUEEN MOTHER, LORD RIVERS, *and* LORD GREY*'*

Rivers. Have patience, madam: there's no doubt his majesty
Will soon recover his accustomed health.

Grey. In that you brook it ill, it makes him worse:
Therefore, for God's sake, entertain good comfort,
And cheer his grace with quick and merry eyes.

Queen Elizabeth. If he were dead, what would betide on me?

Grey. No other harm but loss of such a lord.

Queen Elizabeth. The loss of such a lord includes all harms.

Grey. The heavens have blessed you with a goodly son,
To be your comforter when he is gone.

Queen Elizabeth. Ah, he is young, and his minority
Is put unto the trust of Richard Gloucester,
A man that loves not me, nor none of you.

Rivers. Is it concluded he shall be Protector?

Queen Elizabeth. It is determined, not concluded yet:
But so it must be, if the king miscarry.

Enter BUCKINGHAM *and* STANLEY, EARL OF DERBY

Grey. Here come the lords of Buckingham and Derby.

Buckingham. Good time of day unto your royal grace!

Stanley. God make your majesty joyful as you have been!

Queen Elizabeth. The Countess Richmond, good my Lord of Derby,

To your good prayer will scarcely say amen.
Yet, Derby, notwithstanding she's your wife,
And loves not me, be you, good lord, assured
I hate not you for her proud arrogance.

Stanley. I do beseech you, either not believe
The envious slanders of her false accusers,
Or if she be accused on true report,
Bear with her weakness, which I think proceeds
From wayward sickness, and no grounded malice.

Queen Elizabeth. Saw you the king to-day, my Lord of Derby?

Stanley. But now the Duke of Buckingham and I
Are come from visiting his majesty.

Queen Elizabeth. What likelihood of his amendment, lords?

Buckingham. Madam, good hope; his grace speaks cheerfully.

Queen Elizabeth. God grant him health! Did you confer with him?

Buckingham. Ay, madam: he desires to make atonement
Between the Duke of Gloucester and your brothers,
And between them and my Lord Chamberlain;
And sent to warn them to his royal presence.

Queen Elizabeth. Would all were well! but that will never be:
I fear our happiness is at the height.

Enter GLOUCESTER, HASTINGS, *and* DERBY

Gloucester. They do me wrong, and I will not endure it.
Who is it that complains unto the king,
That I, forsooth, am stern and love them not?
By holy Paul, they love his grace but lightly
That fill his ears with such dissentious rumours.

Because I cannot flatter and look fair,
Smile in men's faces, smooth, deceive and cog,
Duck with French nods and apish courtesy,
I must be held a rancorous enemy.
Cannot a plain man live and think no harm,
But thus his simple truth must be abused
With silken, sly, insinuating Jacks?

Grey. To whom in all this presence speaks your grace?

Gloucester. To thee, that hast nor honesty nor grace.
When have I injured thee? when done thee wrong?
Or thee? or thee? or any of your faction?
A plague upon you all! His royal grace
(Whom God preserve better than you would wish!)
Cannot be quiet scarce a breathing while,
But you must trouble him with lewd complaints.

Queen Elizabeth. Brother of Gloucester, you mistake the matter.
The king, on his own royal disposition
(And not provoked by any suitor else),
Aiming, belike, at your interior hatred,
That in your outward action shows itself
Against my children, brothers, and myself,
Makes him to send, that he may learn the ground
Of your ill-will, and thereby to remove it.

Gloucester. I cannot tell: the world is grown so bad,
That wrens make prey where eagles dare not perch:
Since every Jack became a gentleman,
There's many a gentle person made a Jack.

Queen Elizabeth. Come, come, we know your meaning, brother Gloucester;
You envy my advancement and my friends':
God grant we never may have need of you!

Gloucester. Meantime, God grants that I have need of you:

Our brother is imprisoned by your means,
Myself disgraced, and the nobility
Held in contempt, while great promotions
Are daily given to ennoble those
That scarce some two days since were worth a noble.
Queen Elizabeth. By Him that raised me to this careful height
From that contented hap which I enjoyed,
I never did incense his majesty
Against the Duke of Clarence, but have been
An earnest advocate to plead for him.
My lord, you do me shameful injury,
Falsely to draw me in these vile suspects.
Gloucester. You may deny that you were not the mean
Of my Lord Hastings' late imprisonment.
Rivers. She may, my lord, for—
Gloucester. She may, Lord Rivers! why, who knows not so?
She may do more, sir, than denying that:
She may help you to many fair preferments
And then deny her aiding hand therein,
And lay those honours on your high desert.
What may she not? She may—ay, marry, may she—
Rivers. What, marry, may she?
Gloucester. What, marry, may she! Marry with a king,
A bachelor, and a handsome stripling too:
Iwis your grandam had a worser match.
Queen Elizabeth. My Lord of Gloucester, I have too long borne
Your blunt upbraidings and your bitter scoffs:
By heaven, I will acquaint his majesty
Of those gross taunts that oft I have endured.
I had rather be a country servant-maid

Than a great queen, with this condition,
To be so baited, scorned, and stormèd at.

'Enter old QUEEN MARGARET*', behind*

Small joy have I in being England's queen.
(*Queen Margaret.* And less'nèd be that small, God I beseech him!
Thy honour, state, and seat is due to me.
Gloucester. What! threat you me with telling of the king?
Tell him, and spare not: look what I have said
I will avouch't in presence of the king:
I dare adventure to be sent to th'Tower.
'Tis time to speak; my pains are quite forgot.
(*Queen Margaret.* Out, devil! I do remember them too well:
Thou kill'dst my husband Henry in the Tower,
And Edward, my poor son, at Tewkesbury.
Gloucester. Ere you were queen, ay, or your husband king,
I was a pack-horse in his great affairs;
A weeder-out of his proud adversaries,
A liberal rewarder of his friends:
To royalise his blood I spent mine own.
(*Queen Margaret.* Ay, and much better blood than his or thine.
Gloucester. In all which time you and your husband Grey
Were factious for the house of Lancaster;
And, Rivers, so were you. Was not your husband
In Margaret's battle at Saint Albans slain?
Let me put in your minds, if you forget,
What you have been ere this, and what you are;
Withal, what I have been, and what I am.

(*Queen Margaret.* A murd'rous villain, and so still thou art.
Gloucester. Poor Clarence did forsake his father, Warwick;
Ay, and forswore himself,—which Jesu pardon!—
(*Queen Margaret.* Which God revenge!
Gloucester. To fight on Edward's party for the crown;
And for his meed, poor lord, he is mewed up.
I would to God my heart were flint, like Edward's,
Or Edward's soft and pitiful, like mine:
I am too childish-foolish for this world.
(*Queen Margaret.* Hie thee to hell for shame and leave this world,
Thou cacodemon! there thy kingdom is.
Rivers. My Lord of Gloucester, in those busy days
Which here you urge to prove us enemies,
We followed then our lord, our sovereign king:
So should we you, if you should be our king.
Gloucester. If I should be! I had rather be a pedlar:
Far be it from my heart, the thought thereof!
Queen Elizabeth. As little joy, my lord, as you suppose
You should enjoy, were you this country's king,
As little joy you may suppose in me
That I enjoy, being the queen thereof.
(*Queen Margaret.* As little joy enjoys the queen thereof;
For I am she, and altogether joyless
I can no longer hold me patient.
[*aloud, advancing*
Hear me, you wrangling pirates, that fall out
In sharing that which you have pilled from me!
Which of you trembles not that looks on me?
If not that I am queen you bow like subjects,

Yet that, by you deposed, you quake like rebels?
Ah, gentle villain, do not turn away!
Gloucester. Foul wrinklèd witch, what mak'st thou in my sight?
Queen Margaret. But repetition of what thou hast marred;
That will I make before I let thee go.
Gloucester. Wert thou not banishèd on pain of death?
Queen Margaret. I was; but I do find more pain in banishment
Than death can yield me here by my abode.
A husband and a son thou ow'st to me;
And thou a kingdom; all of you allegiance:
This sorrow that I have, by right is yours,
And all the pleasures you usurp are mine.
Gloucester. The curse my noble father laid on thee,
When thou didst crown his warlike brows with paper
And with thy scorns drew'st rivers from his eyes,
And then, to dry them, gav'st the duke a clout
Steeped in the faultless blood of pretty Rutland—
His curses, then from bitterness of soul
Denounced against thee, are all fall'n upon thee;
And God, not we, hath plagued thy bloody deed.
Queen Elizabeth. So just is God, to right the innocent.
Hastings. O, 'twas the foulest deed to slay that babe,
And the most merciless that e'er was heard of!
Rivers. Tyrants themselves wept when it was reported.
Dorset. No man but prophesied revenge for it.
Buckingham. Northumberland, then present, wept to see it.
Queen Margaret. What! were you snarling all before I came,
Ready to catch each other by the throat,

And turn you all your hatred now on me?
Did York's dread curse prevail so much with heaven
That Henry's death, my lovely Edward's death,
Their kingdom's loss, my woeful banishment,
Should all but answer for that peevish brat?
Can curses pierce the clouds and enter heaven?
Why, then, give way, dull clouds, to my quick curses!
Though not by war, by surfeit die your king,
As ours, by murder, to make him a king!
Edward thy son, that now is Prince of Wales,
For Edward our son, that was Prince of Wales,
Die in his youth by like untimely violence!
Thyself a queen, for me that was a queen,
Outlive thy glory, like my wretched self!
Long mayst thou live to wail thy children's death;
And see another, as I see thee now,
Decked in thy rights, as thou art stalled in mine!
Long die thy happy days before thy death;
And, after many length'ned hours of grief,
Die neither mother, wife, nor England's queen!
Rivers and Dorset, you were standers by,
And so wast thou, Lord Hastings, when my son
Was stabbed with bloody daggers: God I pray him,
That none of you may live his natural age,
But by some unlooked accident cut off!

Gloucester. Have done thy charm, thou hateful withered hag!

Queen Margaret. And leave out thee? stay, dog, for thou shalt hear me.
If heaven have any grievous plague in store
Exceeding those that I can wish upon thee,
O, let them keep it till thy sins be ripe,
And then hurl down their indignation
On thee, the troubler of the poor world's peace!

The worm of conscience still begnaw thy soul!
Thy friends suspect for traitors while thou liv'st,
And take deep traitors for thy dearest friends!
No sleep close up that deadly eye of thine,
Unless it be while some tormenting dream
Affrights thee with a hell of ugly devils!
Thou elvish-marked, abortive, rooting hog!
Thou that wast sealed in thy nativity
The slave of nature and the son of hell!
Thou slander of thy heavy mother's womb!
Thou loathéd issue of thy father's loins!
Thou rag of honour! thou detested—

Gloucester. Margaret.

Queen Margaret. Richard!

Gloucester. Ha?

Queen Margaret. I call thee not.

Gloucester. I cry thee mercy then, for I did think
That thou hadst called me all these bitter names.

Queen Margaret. Why, so I did, but looked for no reply.
O, let me make the period to my curse!

Gloucester. 'Tis done by me, and ends in 'Margaret'.

Queen Elizabeth. Thus have you breathed your curse against yourself.

Queen Margaret. Poor painted queen, vain flourish of my fortune!
Why strew'st thou sugar on that bottled spider,
Whose deadly web ensnareth thee about?
Fool, fool! thou whet'st a knife to kill thyself.
The day will come that thou shalt wish for me
To help thee curse this poisonous bunch-backed toad.

Hastings. False-boding woman, end thy frantic curse,
Lest to thy harm thou move our patience.

Queen Margaret. Foul shame upon you! you have all moved mine.
Rivers. Were you well served, you would be taught your duty.
Queen Margaret. To serve me well, you all should do me duty,
Teach me to be your queen, and you my subjects:
O, serve me well, and teach yourselves that duty!
Dorset. Dispute not with her; she is lunatic.
Queen Margaret. Peace, master marquis, you are malapert:
Your fire-new stamp of honour is scarce current.
O, that your young nobility could judge
What 'twere to lose it, and be miserable!
They that stand high have many blasts to shake them;
And if they fall, they dash themselves to pieces.
Gloucester. Good counsel, marry: learn it, learn it, marquis.
Dorset. It touches you, my lord, as much as me.
Gloucester. Ay, and much more: but I was born so high,
Our aery buildeth in the cedar's top,
And dallies with the wind, and scorns the sun.
Queen Margaret. And turns the sun to shade; alas! alas!
Witness my son, now in the shade of death;
Whose bright out-shining beams thy cloudy wrath
Hath in eternal darkness folded up.
Your aery buildeth in our aery's nest.
O God, that seest it, do not suffer it;
As it is won with blood, lost be it so!
Gloucester. Peace, peace! for shame, if not for charity.
Queen Margaret. Urge neither charity nor shame to me:

Uncharitably with me have you dealt,
And shamefully my hopes by you are butchered.
My charity is outrage, life my shame;
And in that shame still live my sorrow's rage!
Buckingham. Have done, have done.
Queen Margaret. O princely Buckingham, I'll kiss thy hand,
In sign of league and amity with thee:
Now fair befall thee and thy noble house!
Thy garments are not spotted with our blood,
Nor thou within the compass of my curse.
Buckingham. Nor no one here; for curses never pass
The lips of those that breathe them in the air.
Queen Margaret. I will not think but they ascend the sky,
And there awake God's gentle-sleeping peace.
[*aside*] O Buckingham, take heed of yonder dog!
Look when he fawns, he bites; and when he bites,
His venom tooth will rankle to the death:
Have not to do with him, beware of him;
Sin, death, and hell have set their marks on him,
And all their ministers attend on him.
Gloucester. What doth she say, my Lord of Buckingham?
Buckingham. Nothing that I respect, my gracious lord.
Queen Margaret. What, dost thou scorn me for my gentle counsel?
And soothe the devil that I warn thee from?
O, but remember this another day,
When he shall split thy very heart with sorrow,
And say poor Margaret was a prophetess.
Live each of you the subjects to his hate,
And he to yours, and all of you to God's! [*she goes*

Hastings. My hair doth stand an end to hear her curses.

Rivers. And so doth mine: I muse why she's at liberty.

Gloucester. I cannot blame her: by God's holy mother,
She hath had too much wrong; and I repent
My part thereof that I have done to her.

Queen Elizabeth. I never did her any, to my knowledge.

Gloucester. Yet you have all the vantage of her wrong.
I was too hot to do somebody good,
That is too cold in thinking of it now.
Marry, for Clarence, he is well repaid;
He is franked up to fatting for his pains:
God pardon them that are the cause thereof!

Rivers. A virtuous and a Christian-like conclusion,
To pray for them that have done scathe to us!

Gloucester. So do I ever—['*speaks to himself*'] being well advised,
For had I cursed now, I had cursed myself.

'*Enter* CATESBY'

Catesby. Madam, his majesty doth call for you;
And for your grace; and you, my gracious lords.

Queen Elizabeth. Catesby, I come. Lords, will you go with me?

Rivers. We wait upon your grace.
['*all but Gloucester*' *go*

Gloucester. I do the wrong, and first begin to brawl.
The secret mischiefs that I set abroach
I lay unto the grievous charge of others.
Clarence, whom I, indeed, have cast in darkness,
I do beweep to many simple gulls;

Namely to Derby, Hastings, Buckingham;
And tell them 'tis the queen and her allies
That stir the king against the duke my brother.
Now, they believe it; and withal whet me
To be revenged on Rivers, Dorset, Grey:
But then I sigh; and, with a piece of Scripture,
Tell them that God bids us do good for evil:
And thus I clothe my naked villany
With odd old ends stol'n forth of Holy Writ;
And seem a saint, when most I play the devil.

'Enter two Murderers'

But soft! here come my executioners.
How now, my hardy stout resolvéd mates!
Are you now going to dispatch this thing?

1 *Murderer.* We are, my lord, and come to have the warrant,
That we may be admitted where he is.

Gloucester. Well thought upon, I have it here about me. [*gives the warrant*
When you have done, repair to Crosby Place.
But, sirs, be sudden in the execution,
Withal obdurate, do not hear him plead;
For Clarence is well-spoken, and perhaps
May move your hearts to pity, if you mark him.

1 *Murderer.* Tut, tut, my lord, we will not stand to prate;
Talkers are no good doers: be assured
We go to use our hands and not our tongues.

Gloucester. Your eyes drop millstones, when fools' eyes fall tears.
I like you, lads: about your business straight.
Go, go, dispatch.

1 *Murderer.* We will, my noble lord. [*they go*

[1.4.] *London. The Tower*

Enter CLARENCE *and* BRAKENBURY

Brakenbury. Why looks your grace so heavily to-day?
Clarence. O, I have passed a miserable night,
So full of fearful dreams, of ugly sights,
That, as I am a Christian faithful man,
I would not spend another such a night,
Though 'twere to buy a world of happy days,
So full of dismal terror was the time!
Brakenbury. What was your dream, my lord? I pray you tell me.
Clarence. Methoughts that I had broken from the Tower,
And was embarked to cross to Burgundy,
And in my company my brother Gloucester,
Who from my cabin tempted me to walk
Upon the hatches. Thence we looked toward England,
And cited up a thousand heavy times,
During the wars of York and Lancaster
That had befall'n us. As we paced along
Upon the giddy footing of the hatches,
Methought that Gloucester stumbled, and in falling
Struck me, that thought to stay him, overboard,
Into the tumbling billows of the main.
O Lord, methought what pain it was to drown!
What dreadful noise of waters in mine ears!
What sights of ugly death within mine eyes!
Methoughts I saw a thousand fearful wracks;
A thousand men that fishes gnawed upon;
Wedges of gold, great ingots, heaps of pearl,
Inestimable stones, unvalued jewels,
All scatt'red in the bottom of the sea.

Some lay in dead men's skulls; and in the holes
Where eyes did once inhabit there were crept,
As 'twere in scorn of eyes, reflecting gems,
That wooed the slimy bottom of the deep,
And mocked the dead bones that lay scatt'red by.
Brakenbury. Had you such leisure in the time of death
To gaze upon these secrets of the deep?
Clarence. Methought I had; and often did I strive
To yield the ghost: but still the envious flood
Stopped in my soul, and would not let it forth
To find the empty, vast, and wand'ring air;
But smothered it within my panting bulk,
Who almost burst to belch it in the sea.
Brakenbury. Awaked you not in this sore agony?
Clarence. No, no, my dream was lengthened after life.
O, then began the tempest to my soul.
I passed, methought, the melancholy flood,
With that sour ferryman which poets write of,
Unto the kingdom of perpetual night.
The first that there did greet my stranger soul,
Was my great father-in-law, renownéd Warwick;
Who spake aloud, 'What scourge for perjury
Can this dark monarchy afford false Clarence?'
And so he vanished. Then came wand'ring by
A shadow like an angel, with bright hair
Dabbled in blood, and he shrieked out aloud,
'Clarence is come; false, fleeting, perjured Clarence,
That stabbed me in the field by Tewkesbury:
Seize on him, Furies, take him unto torment!'
With that, methought, a legion of foul fiends
Environed me, and howléd in mine ears

Such hideous cries that with the very noise
I trembling waked, and for a season after
Could not believe but that I was in hell,
Such terrible impression made my dream.

Brakenbury. No marvel, lord, though it affrighted you;
I am afraid, methinks, to hear you tell it.

Clarence. Ah, Keeper, Keeper, I have done these things,
That now give evidence against my soul,
For Edward's sake, and see how he requits me!
O God! if my deep prayers cannot appease thee,
But thou wilt be avenged on my misdeeds,
Yet execute thy wrath in me alone;
O, spare my guiltless wife and my poor children!
Keeper, I prithee, sit by me awhile,
My soul is heavy, and I fain would sleep.

Brakenbury. I will, my lord: God give your grace good rest! [*Clarence sleeps*
Sorrow breaks seasons and reposing hours,
Makes the night morning and the noon-tide night.
Princes have but their titles for their glories,
An outward honour for an inward toil;
And for unfelt imaginations
They often feel a world of restless cares:
So that between their titles and low name
There's nothing differs but the outward fame.

Enter the two Murderers

1 *Murderer.* Ho! who's here?

Brakenbury. What wouldst thou, fellow? and how cam'st thou hither?

1 *Murderer.* I would speak with Clarence, and I came hither on my legs.

Brakenbury. What, so brief?

2 *Murderer*. 'Tis better, sir, than to be tedious.
Let him see our commission, and talk no more.
[*Brakenbury 'reads' it*

Brakenbury. I am in this commanded to deliver
The noble Duke of Clarence to your hands.
I will not reason what is meant hereby,
Because I will be guiltless from the meaning.
There lies the duke asleep, and there the keys.
I'll to the king, and signify to him
That thus I have resigned to you my charge.

1 *Murderer*. You may, sir; 'tis a point of wisdom: fare you well. [*Brakenbury goes*

2 *Murderer*. What, shall I stab him as he sleeps?

1 *Murderer*. No; he'll say 'twas done cowardly, when he wakes.

2 *Murderer*. Why, he shall never wake until the great judgement-day.

1 *Murderer*. Why, then he'll say we stabbed him sleeping.

2 *Murderer*. The urging of that word 'judgement' hath bred a kind of remorse in me.

1 *Murderer*. What, art thou afraid?

2 *Murderer*. Not to kill him, having a warrant; but to be damned for killing him, from the which no warrant can defend me.

1 *Murderer*. I thought thou hadst been resolute.

2 *Murderer*. So I am, to let him live.

1 *Murderer*. I'll back to the Duke of Gloucester, and tell him so.

2 *Murderer*. Nay, I prithee, stay a little: I hope this passionate humour of mine will change; it was wont to hold me but while one tells twenty.

1 *Murderer*. How dost thou feel thyself now?

2 *Murderer.* Faith, some certain dregs of conscience are yet within me.

1 *Murderer.* Remember our reward when the deed's done.

2 *Murderer.* Zounds, he dies: I had forgot the reward.

1 *Murderer.* Where's thy conscience now?

2 *Murderer.* O, in the Duke of Gloucester's purse.

1 *Murderer.* When he opens his purse to give us our reward, thy conscience flies out.

2 *Murderer.* 'Tis no matter, let it go; there's few or none will entertain it.

1 *Murderer.* What if it come to thee again?

2 *Murderer.* I'll not meddle with it: it makes a man a coward: a man cannot steal, but it accuseth him; a man cannot swear, but it checks him; a man cannot lie with his neighbour's wife, but it detects him: 'tis a blushing shamefaced spirit that mutinies in a man's bosom; it fills a man full of obstacles. It made me once restore a purse of gold, that (by chance) I found; it beggars any man that keeps it: it is turned out of towns and cities for a dangerous thing; and every man that means to live well endeavours to trust to himself and live without it.

1 *Murderer.* 'Tis even now at my elbow, persuading me not to kill the duke.

2 *Murderer.* Take the devil in thy mind, and believe him not: he would insinuate with thee but to make thee sigh.

1 *Murderer.* I am strong-framed, he cannot prevail with me.

2 *Murderer.* Spoke like a tall man that respects thy reputation. Come, shall we fall to work?

1 *Murderer.* Take him on the costard with the hilts

of thy sword, and then throw him into the malmsey-butt in the next room.

2 *Murderer*. O excellent device! and make a sop of him.

1 *Murderer*. Soft! he wakes.

2 *Murderer*. Strike!

1 *Murderer*. No, we'll reason with him.

Clarence. Where art thou, Keeper? give me a cup of wine.

2 *Murderer*. You shall have wine enough, my lord, anon.

Clarence. In God's name, what art thou?

1 *Murderer*. A man, as you are.

Clarence. But not, as I am, royal.

2 *Murderer*. Nor you, as we are, loyal.

Clarence. Thy voice is thunder, but thy looks are humble.

1 *Murderer*. My voice is now the king's, my looks mine own.

Clarence. How darkly and how deadly dost thou speak!
Your eyes do menace me: why look you pale?
Who sent you hither? Wherefore do you come?

2 *Murderer*. To, to, to—

Clarence. To murder me?

Both. Ay, ay.

Clarence. You scarcely have the hearts to tell me so,
And therefore cannot have the hearts to do it.
Wherein, my friends, have I offended you?

1 *Murderer*. Offended us you have not, but the king.

Clarence. I shall be reconciled to him again.

2 *Murderer*. Never, my lord; therefore prepare to die.

Clarence. Are you drawn forth, among a world of men

To slay the innocent? What is my offence?
Where is the evidence that doth accuse me?
What lawful quest have given their verdict up
Unto the frowning judge? or who pronounced
The bitter sentence of poor Clarence' death?
Before I be convict by course of law,
To threaten me with death is most unlawful.
I charge you, as you hope to have redemption
By Christ's dear blood shed for our grievous sins,
That you depart and lay no hands on me:
The deed you undertake is damnable.

1 *Murderer*. What we will do, we do upon command.

2 *Murderer*. And he that hath commanded is our king.

Clarence. Erroneous vassals! the great King of kings
Hath in the tables of his law commanded
That thou shalt do no murder: will you then
Spurn at his edict, and fulfil a man's?
Take heed; for he holds vengeance in his hand,
To hurl upon their heads that break his law.

2 *Murderer*. And that same vengeance doth he hurl on thee,
For false forswearing, and for murder too:
Thou didst receive the sacrament to fight
In quarrel of the house of Lancaster.

1 *Murderer*. And, like a traitor to the name of God,
Didst break that vow, and with thy treacherous blade
Unrip'st the bowels of thy sov'reign's son.

2 *Murderer*. Whom thou wast sworn to cherish and defend.

1 *Murderer*. How canst thou urge God's dreadful law to us,
When thou hast broke it in such dear degree?

Clarence. Alas! for whose sake did I that ill deed?
For Edward, for my brother, for his sake.

He sends you not to murder me for this;
For in that sin he is as deep as I.
If God will be avengéd for the deed,
O, know you yet he doth it publicly.
Take not the quarrel from his powerful arm;
He needs no indirect or lawless course
To cut off those that have offended him.

1 *Murderer*. Who made thee then a bloody minister,
When gallant-springing brave Plantagenet,
That princely novice, was struck dead by thee?

Clarence. My brother's love, the devil, and my rage.

1 *Murderer*. Thy brother's love, our duty, and thy faults,
Provoke us hither now to slaughter thee.

Clarence. If you do love my brother, hate not me;
I am his brother, and I love him well.
If you are hired, for meed go back again,
And I will send you to my brother Gloucester,
Who shall reward you better for my life
Than Edward will for tidings of my death.

2 *Murderer*. You are deceived, your brother Gloucester hates you.

Clarence. O, no, he loves me, and he holds me dear:
Go you to him from me.

1 *Murderer*. Ay, so we will.

Clarence. Tell him, when that our princely father York
Blessed his three sons with his victorious arm,
And charged us from his soul to love each other,
He little thought of this divided friendship:
Bid Gloucester think of this, and he will weep.

1 *Murderer*. Ay, millstones, as he lessoned us to weep.

Clarence. O, do not slander him, for he is kind.

1 *Murderer*. As snow in harvest. Come, you deceive yourself:
'Tis he that sends us to destroy you here.
Clarence. It cannot be; for he bewept my fortune,
And hugged me in his arms, and swore with sobs,
That he would labour my delivery.
1 *Murderer*. Why, so he doth, when he delivers you
From this earth's thraldom to the joys of heaven.
2 *Murderer*. Make peace with God, for you must die, my lord.
Clarence. Have you that holy feeling in your souls,
To counsel me to make my peace with God,
And are you yet to your own souls so blind,
That you will war with God by murd'ring me?
O, sirs, consider, they that set you on
To do this deed will hate you for the deed.
2 *Murderer*. What shall we do?
Clarence. Relent, and save your souls.
Which of you, if you were a prince's son,
Being pent from liberty, as I am now,
If two such murderers as yourselves came to you,
Would not entreat for life? Even so I beg
As you would beg, were you in my distress.
1 *Murderer*. Relent! 'tis cowardly and womanish.
Clarence. Not to relent is beastly, savage, devilish.
My friend, [*to* 2 *Murderer*] I spy some pity in thy looks;
O, if thine eye be not a flatterer,
Come thou on my side, and entreat for me.
A begging prince what beggar pities not?
2 *Murderer*. Look behind you, my lord.
1 *Murderer*. ['*stabs him*'] Take that, and that: if all this will not do,
I'll drown you in the malmsey-butt within.
[*drags out the body*

2 *Murderer*. A bloody deed, and desperately dispatched!
How fain, like Pilate, would I wash my hands
Of this most grievous murder!

1 Murderer returns

1 *Murderer*. How now! what mean'st thou, that thou help'st me not?
By heavens, the duke shall know how slack you have been!
2 *Murderer*. I would he knew that I had saved his brother!
Take thou the fee, and tell him what I say,
For I repent me that the duke is slain. [*goes*
1 *Murderer*. So do not I: go, coward as thou art.
Well, I'll go hide the body in some hole,
Till that the duke give order for his burial:
And when I have my meed, I will away;
For this will out, and then I must not stay. [*goes*

[2. 1.] *London. The palace*

Flourish. Enter KING EDWARD *sick, borne in a chair, with* QUEEN ELIZABETH, DORSET, RIVERS, HASTINGS, BUCKINGHAM, GREY, *and others.*

King Edward. Why, so: now have I done a good day's work.
You peers, continue this united league:
I every day expect an embassage
From my Redeemer to redeem me hence;
And more at peace my soul shall part to heaven,
Since I have made my friends at peace on earth.

Hastings and Rivers, take each other's hand;
Dissemble not your hatred, swear your love.
Rivers. By heaven, my soul is purged from grudging hate;
And with my hand I seal my true heart's love.
Hastings. So thrive I, as I truly swear the like!
King Edward. Take heed you dally not before your king;
Lest he that is the supreme King of kings
Confound your hidden falsehood and award
Either of you to be the other's end.
Hastings. So prosper I, as I swear perfect love!
Rivers. And I, as I love Hastings with my heart!
King Edward. Madam, yourself is not exempt from this,
Nor you, son Dorset; Buckingham, nor you;
You have been factious one against the other.
Wife, love Lord Hastings, let him kiss your hand;
And what you do, do it unfeignedly.
Queen Elizabeth. There, Hastings; I will never more remember
Our former hatred, so thrive I and mine!
King Edward. Dorset, embrace him; Hastings, love lord marquis.
Dorset. This interchange of love, I here protest,
Upon my part shall be inviolable.
Hastings. And so swear I. [*they embrace*
King Edward. Now, princely Buckingham, seal thou this league
With thy embracements to my wife's allies,
And make me happy in your unity.
Buckingham. [*to the Queen*] Whenever Buckingham doth turn his hate
Upon your grace, but with all duteous love

Doth cherish you and yours, God punish me
With hate in those where I expect most love!
When I have most need to employ a friend,
And most assuréd that he is a friend,
Deep, hollow, treacherous and full of guile,
Be he unto me! this do I beg of God,
When I am cold in love to you or yours.

[*they* '*embrace*'

King Edward. A pleasing cordial, princely Buckingham,
Is this thy vow unto my sickly heart.
There wanteth now our brother Gloucester here,
To make the blessed period of this peace.

Buckingham. And in good time,
Here comes Sir Richard Ratcliffe and the duke.

Enter GLOUCESTER *and* RATCLIFFE

Gloucester. Good morrow to my sovereign king and queen;
And, princely peers, a happy time of day!

King Edward. Happy indeed, as we have spent the day.
Gloucester, we have done deeds of charity,
Made peace of enmity, fair love of hate,
Between these swelling wrong-incenséd peers.

Gloucester. A blesséd labour, my most sovereign lord.
Among this princely heap, if any here,
By false intelligence, or wrong surmise,
Hold me a foe; if I unwittingly
Have aught committed that is hardly borne
By any in this presence, I desire
To reconcile me to his friendly peace:
'Tis death to me to be at enmity;
I hate it, and desire all good men's love.

First, madam, I entreat true peace of you,
Which I will purchase with my duteous service;
Of you, my noble cousin Buckingham,
If ever any grudge were lodged between us;
Of you, and you, Lord Rivers, and Lord Dorset,
Of you, Lord Woodeville and Lord Scales of you,
That all without desert have frowned on me;
Dukes, earls, lords, gentlemen; indeed, of all.
I do not know that Englishman alive
With whom my soul is any jot at odds
More than the infant that is born to-night:
I thank my God for my humility.

Queen Elizabeth. A holy day shall this be kept hereafter:
I would to God all strifes were well compounded.
My sovereign lord, I do beseech your highness
To take our brother Clarence to your grace.

Gloucester. Why, madam, have I off'red love for this,
To be so flouted in this royal presence?
Who knows not that the gentle duke is dead?
['*they all start*'
You do him injury to scorn his corse.

Rivers. Who knows not he is dead! who knows he is?

Queen Elizabeth. All-seeing heaven, what a world is this!

Buckingham. Look I so pale, Lord Dorset, as the rest?

Dorset. Ay, my good lord, and no man in the presence
But his red colour hath forsook his cheeks.

King Edward. Is Clarence dead? the order was reversed.

Gloucester. But he, poor man, by your first order died,
And that a wingéd Mercury did bear;
Some tardy cripple bare the countermand
That came too lag to see him buriéd.

God grant that some, less noble and less loyal,
Nearer in bloody thoughts, but not in blood,
Deserve not worse than wretched Clarence did,
And yet go current from suspicion!

Enter LORD STANLEY

Stanley. A boon, my sovereign, for my service done!
King Edward. I prithee, peace: my soul is full of sorrow.
Stanley. I will not rise, unless your highness hear me.
King Edward. Then say at once what is it thou requests.
Stanley. The forfeit, sovereign, of my servant's life;
Who slew to-day a riotous gentleman
Lately attendant on the Duke of Norfolk.
King Edward. Have I a tongue to doom my brother's death,
And shall that tongue give pardon to a slave?
My brother killed no man—his fault was thought,
And yet his punishment was bitter death.
Who sued to me for him? who, in my wrath,
Kneeled at my feet and bid me be advised?
Who spoke of brotherhood? who spoke of love?
Who told me how the poor soul did forsake
The mighty Warwick, and did fight for me?
Who told me, in the field at Tewkesbury
When Oxford had me down, he rescued me
And said 'Dear brother, live, and be a king'?
Who told me, when we both lay in the field
Frozen almost to death, how he did lap me
Even in his garments, and did give himself,
All thin and naked, to the numb cold night?
All this from my remembrance brutish wrath

Sinfully plucked, and not a man of you
Had so much grace to put it in my mind.
But when your carters or your waiting-vassals
Have done a drunken slaughter and defaced
The precious image of our dear Redeemer,
You straight are on your knees for pardon, pardon;
And I, unjustly too, must grant it you. [*Stanley rises*
But for my brother not a man would speak,
Nor I, ungracious, speak unto myself
For him, poor soul. The proudest of you all
Have been beholding to him in his life;
Yet none of you would once beg for his life.
O God, I fear thy justice will take hold
On me, and you, and mine, and yours, for this!
Come, Hastings, help me to my closet. Ah,
poor Clarence!
[*he is carried forth; Hastings, the Queen, Rivers, and Dorset in attendance*

Gloucester. This is the fruits of rashness. Marked
you not
How that the guilty kindred of the queen
Looked pale when they did hear of Clarence' death?
O, they did urge it still unto the king!
God will revenge it. Come, lords, will you go
To comfort Edward with our company?

Buckingham. We wait upon your grace. [*they follow*

[2. 2.] '*Enter the old* DUCHESS OF YORK, *with the two children of Clarence*'

Boy. Good grandam, tell us, is our father dead?

Duchess. No, boy.

Girl. Why do you weep so oft, and beat your breast,
And cry 'O Clarence, my unhappy son!'?

Boy. Why do you look on us, and shake your head,

And call us orphans, wretches, castaways,
If that our noble father were alive?
Duchess. My pretty cousins, you mistake me both.
I do lament the sickness of the king,
As loath to lose him, not your father's death;
It were lost sorrow to wail one that's lost.
Boy. Then you conclude, my grandam, he is dead.
The king mine uncle is to blame for it:
God will revenge it, whom I will importune
With earnest prayers, all to that effect.
Girl. And so will I.
Duchess. Peace, children, peace! the king doth love you well.
Incapable and shallow innocents,
You cannot guess who caused your father's death.
Boy. Grandam, we can; for my good uncle Gloucester
Told me the king, provoked to it by the queen,
Devised impeachments to imprison him:
And when my uncle told me so, he wept,
And pitied me, and kindly kissed my cheek;
Bade me rely on him as on my father,
And he would love me dearly as a child.
Duchess. Ah, that deceit should steal such gentle shape,
And with a virtuous vizor hide deep vice!
He is my son, ay, and therein my shame;
Yet from my dugs he drew not this deceit.
Boy. Think you my uncle did dissemble, grandam?
Duchess. Ay, boy.
Boy. I cannot think it. Hark! what noise is this?

'*Enter the* QUEEN *with her hair about her ears,*
RIVERS *and* DORSET *after her*'

Queen Elizabeth. Ah, who shall hinder me to wail and weep,

To chide my fortune and torment myself?
I'll join with black despair against my soul,
And to myself become an enemy.
Duchess. What means this scene of rude impatience?
Queen Elizabeth. To mark an act of tragic violence.
Edward, my lord, thy son, our king, is dead.
Why grow the branches when the root is gone?
Why wither not the leaves that want their sap?
If you will live, lament; if die, be brief,
That our swift-wingéd souls may catch the king's,
Or, like obedient subjects, follow him
To his new kingdom of ne'er-changing night.
Duchess. Ah, so much interest have I in thy sorrow
As I had title in thy noble husband!
I have bewept a worthy husband's death,
And lived with looking on his images:
But now two mirrors of his princely semblance
Are cracked in pieces by malignant death,
And I for comfort have but one false glass,
That grieves me when I see my shame in him.
Thou art a widow; yet thou art a mother,
And hast the comfort of thy children left:
But death hath snatched my husband from mine arms,
And plucked two crutches from my feeble hands,
Clarence and Edward. O, what cause have I,
Thine being but a moiety of my moan,
To overgo thy woes and drown thy cries!
Boy. Ah aunt! you wept not for our father's death,
How can we aid you with our kindred tears?
Girl. Our fatherless distress was left unmoaned;
Your widow-dolour likewise be unwept!
Queen Elizabeth. Give me no help in lamentation;
I am not barren to bring forth complaints:
All springs reduce their currents to mine eyes,

That I, being governed by the watery moon,
May send forth plenteous tears to drown the world!
Ah for my husband, for my dear lord Edward!
Children. Ah for our father, for our dear Lord Clarence!
Duchess. Alas for both, both mine, Edward and Clarence!
Queen Elizabeth. What stay had I but Edward? and he's gone.
Children. What stay had we but Clarence? and he's gone.
Duchess. What stays had I but they? and they are gone.
Queen Elizabeth. Was never widow had so dear a loss.
Children. Were never orphans had so dear a loss.
Duchess. Was never mother had so dear a loss.
Alas, I am the mother of these griefs!
Their woes are parcelled, mine is general.
She for an Edward weeps, and so do I;
I for a Clarence weep, so doth not she:
These babes for Clarence weep, and so do I;
I for an Edward weep, so do not they:
Alas, you three on me, threefold distressed,
Pour all your tears! I am your sorrow's nurse,
And I will pamper it with lamentation.
Dorset. Comfort, dear mother: God is much displeased
That you take with unthankfulness his doing:
In common worldly things 'tis called ungrateful
With dull unwillingness to repay a debt
Which with a bounteous hand was kindly lent;
Much more to be thus opposite with heaven,
For it requires the royal debt it lent you.
Rivers. Madam, bethink you, like a careful mother,

Of the young prince your son: send straight for him;
Let him be crowned; in him your comfort lives.
Drown desperate sorrow in dead Edward's grave,
And plant your joys in living Edward's throne.

Enter GLOUCESTER, BUCKINGHAM, DERBY, HASTINGS, *and* RATCLIFFE

Gloucester. Sister, have comfort: all of us have cause
To wail the dimming of our shining star;
But none can help our harms by wailing them.
Madam, my mother, I do cry you mercy;
I did not see your grace [*he kneels*]. Humbly on my knee
I crave your blessing.
Duchess. God bless thee, and put meekness in thy breast,
Love, charity, obedience, and true duty!
Gloucester. Amen! [*aside*] and make me die a good old man!
That is the butt-end of a mother's blessing:
I marvel that her grace did leave it out.
Buckingham. You cloudy princes and heart-sorrowing peers,
That bear this heavy mutual load of moan,
Now cheer each other in each other's love:
Though we have spent our harvest of this king,
We are to reap the harvest of his son.
The broken rancour of your high-swoln hearts,
But lately splintered, knit, and joined together,
Must gently be preserved, cherished, and kept:
Me seemeth good that, with some little train,
Forthwith from Ludlow the young prince be fet
Hither to London, to be crowned our king.
Rivers. Why with some little train, my Lord of Buckingham?

Buckingham. Marry, my lord, lest by a multitude
The new-healed wound of malice should break out;
Which would be so much the more dangerous,
By how much the estate is green and yet ungoverned:
Where every horse bears his commanding rein,
And may direct his course as please himself,
As well the fear of harm as harm apparent,
In my opinion, ought to be prevented.
Gloucester. I hope the king made peace with all of us;
And the compact is firm and true in me.
Rivers. And so in me; and so, I think, in all.
Yet, since it is but green, it should be put
To no apparent likelihood of breach,
Which haply by much company might be urged:
Therefore I say with noble Buckingham
That it is meet so few should fetch the prince.
Hastings. And so say I.
Gloucester. Then be it so; and go we to determine
Who they shall be that straight shall post to Ludlow.
Madam, and you, my sister, will you go
To give your censures in this business?
Queen Elizabeth. } With all our hearts.
Duchess. }
[*all go in but Buckingham and Gloucester*
Buckingham. My lord, whoever journeys to the prince,
For God sake let not us two stay at home:
For, by the way, I'll sort occasion,
As index to the story we late talked of,
To part the queen's proud kindred from the prince.
Gloucester. My other self, my counsel's consistory,
My oracle, my prophet, my dear cousin!
I, as a child, will go by thy direction.
Toward Ludlow then, for we'll not stay behind.
[*they go*

[2. 3.] *London. A Street*

Enter two Citizens, meeting

1 *Citizen.* Good morrow, neighbour, whither away so fast?
2 *Citizen.* I promise you, I scarcely know myself:
Hear you the news abroad?
1 *Citizen.* Yes, that the king is dead.
2 *Citizen.* Ill news, by'r lady. Seldom comes the better.
I fear, I fear, 'twill prove a giddy world.

'*Enter another Citizen*'

3 *Citizen.* Neighbours, God speed!
1 *Citizen.* Give you good morrow, sir.
3 *Citizen.* Doth the news hold of good King Edward's death?
2 *Citizen.* Ay, sir, it is too true, God help the while!
3 *Citizen.* Then, masters, look to see a troublous world.
1 *Citizen.* No, no; by God's good grace his son shall reign.
3 *Citizen.* Woe to that land that's governed by a child!
2 *Citizen.* In him there is a hope of government,
Which, in his nonage, council under him,
And, in his full and ripened years, himself,
No doubt, shall then, and till then, govern well.
1 *Citizen.* So stood the state when Henry the Sixth
Was crowned in Paris but at nine months old.
3 *Citizen.* Stood the state so? No, no, good friends, God wot;
For then this land was famously enriched

With politic grave counsel; then the king
Had virtuous uncles to protect his grace.

1 *Citizen.* Why, so hath this, both by his father and mother.

3 *Citizen.* Better it were they all came by his father,
Or by his father there were none at all;
For emulation who shall now be nearest,
Will touch us all too near, if God prevent not.
O, full of danger is the Duke of Gloucester!
And the queen's sons and brothers haught and proud:
And were they to be ruled, and not to rule,
This sickly land might solace as before.

1 *Citizen.* Come, come, we fear the worst; all will be well.

3 *Citizen.* When clouds are seen, wise men put on their cloaks;
When great leaves fall, then winter is at hand;
When the sun sets, who doth not look for night?
Untimely storms makes men expect a dearth.
All may be well; but, if God sort it so,
'Tis more than we deserve, or I expect.

2 *Citizen.* Truly, the hearts of men are full of fear:
You cannot reason almost with a man
That looks not heavily and full of dread.

3 *Citizen.* Before the days of change, still is it so:
By a divine instinct men's minds mistrust
Ensuing danger; as by proof we see
The water swell before a boist'rous storm.
But leave it all to God. Whither away?

2 *Citizen.* Marry, we were sent for to the justices.

3 *Citizen.* And so was I: I'll bear you company.

[*they pass on*

[2. 4.] *London. The palace*

Enter the ARCHBISHOP OF YORK, *the young* DUKE OF YORK, QUEEN ELIZABETH, *and the* DUCHESS OF YORK

Archbishop. Last night, I hear, they lay at Stony Stratford;
And at Northampton they do rest to-night:
To-morrow, or next day, they will be here.
Duchess. I long with all my heart to see the prince:
I hope he is much grown since last I saw him.
Queen Elizabeth. But I hear, no; they say my son of York
Has almost overta'en him in his growth.
York. Ay, mother, but I would not have it so.
Duchess. Why, my good cousin, it is good to grow.
York. Grandam, one night, as we did sit at supper,
My uncle Rivers talked how I did grow
More than my brother: 'Ay,' quoth my uncle Gloucester,
'Small herbs have grace, ill weeds do grow apace':
And since, methinks, I would not grow so fast,
Because sweet flowers are slow and weeds make haste.
Duchess. Good faith, good faith, the saying did not hold
In him that did object the same to thee:
He was the wretched'st thing when he was young,
So long a-growing and so leisurely,
That, if his rule were true, he should be gracious.
Archbishop. And so, no doubt, he is, my gracious madam.
Duchess. I hope he is, but yet let mothers doubt.
York. Now, by my troth, if I had been rememb'red,

I could have given my uncle's grace a flout,
To touch his growth nearer than he touched mine.
Duchess. How, my young York? I prithee, let me hear it.
York. Marry, they say my uncle grew so fast
That he could gnaw a crust at two hours old:
'Twas full two years ere I could get a tooth.
Grandam, this would have been a biting jest.
Duchess. I prithee, pretty York, who told thee this?
York. Grandam, his nurse.
Duchess. His nurse! why, she was dead ere thou wast born.
York. If 'twere not she, I cannot tell who told me.
Queen Elizabeth. A parlous boy: go to, you are too shrewd.
Archbishop. Good madam, be not angry with the child.
Queen Elizabeth. Pitchers have ears.

'*Enter a Messenger*'

Archbishop. Here comes a messenger. What news?
Messenger. Such news, my lord, as grieves me to report.
Queen Elizabeth. How doth the prince?
Messenger. Well, madam, and in health.
Duchess. What is thy news?
Messenger. Lord Rivers and Lord Grey
Are sent to Pomfret, and with them
Sir Thomas Vaughan, prisoners.
Duchess. Who hath committed them?
Messenger. The mighty dukes,
Gloucester and Buckingham.
Archbishop. For what offence?
Messenger. The sum of all I can, I have disclosed;

Why or for what the nobles were committed
Is all unknown to me, my gracious lord.
Queen Elizabeth. Ay me, I see the ruin of my house!
The tiger now hath seized the gentle hind;
Insulting tyranny begins to jet
Upon the innocent and aweless throne:
Welcome, destruction, blood, and massacre!
I see, as in a map, the end of all.
Duchess. Accurséd and unquiet wrangling days,
How many of you have mine eyes beheld!
My husband lost his life to get the crown;
And often up and down my sons were tossed,
For me to joy and weep their gain and loss:
And being seated, and domestic broils
Clean overblown, themselves, the conquerors,
Make war upon themselves, brother to brother,
Blood to blood, self to self! Preposterous
And frantic outrage, end thy damnéd spleen;
Or let me die, to look on death no more!
Queen Elizabeth. Come, come, my boy; we will to sanctuary.
Madam, farewell.
Duchess. Stay, I will go with you.
Queen Elizabeth. You have no cause.
Archbishop. My gracious lady, go;
And thither bear your treasure and your goods.
For my part, I'll resign unto your grace
The seal I keep: and so betide to me
As well I tender you and all of yours!
Go, I'll conduct you to the sanctuary. [*they go*

[3. 1.] *London. A street*

'The trumpets sound. Enter the young PRINCE, *the Dukes of* GLOUCESTER *and* BUCKINGHAM, *the Lord* CARDINAL, *with'* CATESBY, *and 'others'*

Buckingham. Welcome, sweet prince, to London, to your chamber.
Gloucester. Welcome, dear cousin, my thoughts' sovereign:
The weary way hath made you melancholy.
Prince. No, uncle; but our crosses on the way
Have made it tedious, wearisome, and heavy:
I want more uncles here to welcome me.
Gloucester. Sweet prince, the untainted virtue of your years
Hath not yet dived into the world's deceit:
Nor more can you distinguish of a man
Than of his outward show, which, God he knows,
Seldom or never jumpeth with the heart.
Those uncles which you want were dangerous;
Your grace attended to their sug'red words,
But looked not on the poison of their hearts:
God keep you from them, and from such false friends!
Prince. God keep me from false friends! but they were none.
Gloucester. My lord, the Mayor of London comes to greet you.

'Enter Lord Mayor', and his train

Mayor. God bless your grace with health and happy days!
Prince. I thank you, good my lord, and thank you all.

I thought my mother and my brother York
Would long ere this have met us on the way:
Fie, what a slug is Hastings, that he comes not
To tell us whether they will come or no!

'Enter LORD HASTINGS*'*

Buckingham. And, in good time, here comes the sweating lord.
Prince. Welcome, my lord: what, will our mother come?
Hastings. On what occasion God he knows, not I,
The queen your mother and your brother York
Have taken sanctuary: the tender prince
Would fain have come with me to meet your grace,
But by his mother was perforce withheld.
Buckingham. Fie, what an indirect and peevish course
Is this of hers! Lord Cardinal, will your grace
Persuade the queen to send the Duke of York
Unto his princely brother presently?
If she deny, Lord Hastings, go with him,
And from her jealous arms pluck him perforce.
Cardinal. My Lord of Buckingham, if my weak oratory
Can from his mother win the Duke of York,
Expect him here; but if she be obdurate
To mild entreaties, God in heaven forbid
We should infringe the holy privilege
Of blessed sanctuary! not for all this land
Would I be guilty of so deep a sin.
Buckingham. You are too senseless-obstinate, my lord,
Too ceremonious and traditional:
Weigh it but with the grossness of this age,
You break not sanctuary in seizing him.

The benefit thereof is always granted
To those whose dealings have deserved the place
And those who have the wit to claim the place:
This prince hath neither claimed it nor deserved it;
Therefore, in mine opinion, cannot have it:
Then, taking him from thence that is not there,
You break no privilege nor charter there.
Oft have I heard of sanctuary men,
But sanctuary children ne'er till now.

Cardinal. My lord, you shall o'er-rule my mind for once.
Come on, Lord Hastings, will you go with me?

Hastings. I go, my lord.

Prince. Good lords, make all the speedy haste you may. [*Cardinal and Hastings depart*
Say, uncle Gloucester, if our brother come,
Where shall we sojourn till our coronation?

Gloucester. Where it seems best unto your royal self.
If I may counsel you, some day or two
Your highness shall repose you at the Tower:
Then where you please, and shall be thought most fit
For your best health and recreation.

Prince. I do not like the Tower, of any place.
Did Julius Caesar build that place, my lord?

Buckingham. He did, my gracious lord, begin that place;
Which, since, succeeding ages have re-edified.

Prince. Is it upon record, or else reported
Successively from age to age, he built it?

Buckingham. Upon record, my gracious lord.

Prince. But say, my lord, it were not regist'red,
Methinks the truth should live from age to age,
As 'twere retailed to all posterity,
Even to the general all-ending day.

(*Gloucester.* So wise so young, they say, do ne'er live long.
Prince. What say you, uncle?
Gloucester. I say, without characters, fame lives long.
[*aside*] Thus, like the formal Vice, Iniquity,
I moralize two meanings in one word.
Prince. That Julius Caesar was a famous man;
With what his valour did enrich his wit,
His wit set down to make his valour live:
Death makes no conquest of this conqueror,
For now he lives in fame, though not in life.
I'll tell you what, my cousin Buckingham—
Buckingham. What, my gracious lord?
Prince. An if I live until I be a man,
I'll win our ancient right in France again,
Or die a soldier, as I lived a king.
(*Gloucester.* Short summers lightly have a forward spring.

HASTINGS and the CARDINAL return with young YORK

Buckingham. Now in good time, here comes the Duke of York.
Prince. Richard of York! how fares our loving brother?
York. Well, my dread lord; so must I call you now.
Prince. Ay, brother, to our grief, as it is yours:
Too late he died that might have kept that title,
Which by his death hath lost much majesty.
Gloucester. How fares our cousin, noble Lord of York?
York. I thank you, gentle uncle. O, my lord,
You said that idle weeds are fast in growth:
The prince my brother hath outgrown me far.

Gloucester. He hath, my lord.
York. And therefore is he idle?
Gloucester. O, my fair cousin, I must not say so.
York. Then he is more beholding to you than I.
Gloucester. He may command me as my sovereign;
But you have power in me as in a kinsman.
York. I pray you, uncle, give me this dagger.
Gloucester. My dagger, little cousin? with all my heart.
Prince. A beggar, brother?
York. Of my kind uncle, that I know will give't,
Being but a toy, which is no grief to give.
Gloucester. A greater gift than that I'll give my cousin.
York. A greater gift! O, that's the sword to it.
Gloucester. Ay, gentle cousin, were it light enough.
York. O, then, I see you'll part but with light gifts;
In weightier things you'll say a beggar nay.
Gloucester. It is too heavy for your grace to wear.
York. I'd weigh it lightly, were it heavier.
Gloucester. What, would you have my weapon, little lord?
York. I would, that I might thank you as you call me.
Gloucester. How?
York. Little.
Prince. My Lord of York will still be cross in talk:
Uncle, your grace knows how to bear with him.
York. You mean, to bear me, not to bear with me:
Uncle, my brother mocks both you and me;
Because that I am little, like an ape,
He thinks that you should bear me on your shoulders.
(*Buckingham.* With what a sharp-provided wit he reasons!

To mitigate the scorn he gives his uncle,
He prettily and aptly taunts himself:
So cunning and so young is wonderful.
Gloucester. My lord, will't please you pass along?
Myself and my good cousin Buckingham
Will to your mother, to entreat of her
To meet you at the Tower and welcome you.
York. What, will you go unto the Tower, my lord?
Prince. My Lord Protector needs will have it so.
York. I shall not sleep in quiet at the Tower.
Gloucester. Why, what should you fear?
York. Marry, my uncle Clarence' angry ghost:
My grandam told me he was murdered there.
Prince. I fear no uncles dead.
Gloucester. Nor none that live, I hope.
Prince. An if they live, I hope I need not fear.
But come, my lord; so with a heavy heart,
Thinking on them, go I unto the Tower.
['*A Sennet.*' *Hastings and the Cardinal accompany the Princes, leaving Gloucester with Buckingham and Catesby*

Buckingham. Think you, my lord, this little prating York
Was not incensèd by his subtle mother
To taunt and scorn you thus opprobriously?
Gloucester. No doubt, no doubt: O, 'tis a parlous boy;
Bold, quick, ingenious, forward, capable:
He is all the mother's, from the top to toe.
Buckingham. Well, let them rest. Come Catesby, thou art sworn
As deeply to effect what we intend,
As closely to conceal what we impart:
Thou know'st our reasons urged upon the way.
What think'st thou? is it not an easy matter

To make Lord William Hastings of our mind,
For the instalment of this noble duke
In the seat royal of this famous isle?
Catesby. He for his father's sake so loves the prince
That he will not be won to aught against him.
Buckingham. What think'st thou then of Stanley? will not he?
Catesby. He will do all in all as Hastings doth.
Buckingham. Well, then, no more but this: go, gentle Catesby,
And, as it were far off, sound thou Lord Hastings
How he doth stand affected to our purpose;
And summon him to-morrow to the Tower,
To sit about the coronation.
If thou dost find him tractable to us,
Encourage him, and tell him all our reasons:
If he be leaden, icy-cold, unwilling,
Be thou so too; and so break off the talk,
And give us notice of his inclination:
For we to-morrow hold divided councils,
Wherein thyself shalt highly be employed.
Gloucester. Commend me to Lord William: tell him, Catesby,
His ancient knot of dangerous adversaries
To-morrow are let blood at Pomfret Castle;
And bid my lord, for joy of this good news,
Give Mistress Shore one gentle kiss the more.
Buckland. Good Catesby, go, effect this business soundly.
Catesby. My good lords both, with all the heed I can.
Gloucester. Shall we hear from you, Catesby, ere we sleep?
Catesby. You shall, my lord.

Gloucester. At Crosby House, there shall you find us both. [*Catesby goes*

Buckingham. My lord, what shall we do, if we perceive
Lord Hastings will not yield to our complots?

Gloucester. Chop off his head—something we will determine.
And look when I am king, claim thou of me
The earldom of Hereford, and all the movables
Whereof the king my brother was possessed.

Buckingham. I'll claim that promise at your grace's hand.

Gloucester. And look to have it yielded with all kindness.
Come, let us sup betimes, that afterwards
We may digest our complots in some form. [*they go*

[3. 2.] *Before Lord Hastings' house; night*

'*Enter a Messenger to the door of Hastings*'

Messenger. [*knocks*] My lord! my lord!

Hastings. [*within*] Who knocks?

Messenger. One from the Lord Stanley.

Hastings. [*within*] What is't o'clock?

Messenger. Upon the stroke of four.
[*Hastings opens the door*

Hastings. Cannot my Lord Stanley sleep these tedious nights?

Messenger. So it appears by that I have to say.
First, he commends him to your noble self.

Hastings. What then?

Messenger. Then certifies your lordship that this night
He dreamt the boar had razéd off his helm:

Besides, he says there are two councils kept;
And that may be determined at the one
Which may make you and him to rue at th'other.
Therefore he sends to know your lordship's pleasure—
If you will presently take horse with him,
And with all speed post with him toward the north,
To shun the danger that his soul divines.

Hastings. Go, fellow, go, return unto thy lord;
Bid him not fear the separated councils:
His honour and myself are at the one,
And at the other is my good friend Catesby;
Where nothing can proceed that toucheth us
Whereof I shall not have intelligence.
Tell him his fears are shallow, without instance:
And for his dreams, I wonder he's so simple
To trust the mock'ry of unquiet slumbers.
To fly the boar before the boar pursues
Were to incense the boar to follow us
And make pursuit where he did mean no chase.
Go, bid thy master rise and come to me;
And we will both together to the Tower,
Where he shall see the boar will use us kindly.

Messenger. I'll go, my lord, and tell him what you say. [*goes*

'*Enter* CATESBY'

Catesby. Many good morrows to my noble lord!

Hastings. Good morrow, Catesby, you are early stirring:
What news, what news, in this our tott'ring state?

Catesby. It is a reeling world indeed, my lord;
And I believe will never stand upright
Till Richard wear the garland of the realm.

Hastings. How, wear the garland? dost thou mean the crown?

Catesby. Ay, my good lord.
Hastings. I'll have this crown of mine cut from my shoulders
Before I'll see the crown so foul misplaced.
But canst thou guess that he doth aim at it?
Catesby. Ay, on my life, and hopes to find you forward
Upon his party for the gain thereof:
And thereupon he sends you this good news,
That this same very day your enemies,
The kindred of the queen, must die at Pomfret.
Hastings. Indeed, I am no mourner for that news,
Because they have been still my adversaries:
But, that I'll give my voice on Richard's side,
To bar my master's heirs in true descent,
God knows I will not do it, to the death.
Catesby. God keep your lordship in that gracious mind!
Hastings. But I shall laugh at this a twelve-month hence,
That they which brought me in my master's hate,
I live to look upon their tragedy.
Well, Catesby, ere a fortnight make me older,
I'll send some packing that yet think not on't.
Catesby. 'Tis a vile thing to die, my gracious lord,
When men are unprepared and look not for it.
Hastings. O monstrous, monstrous! and so falls it out
With Rivers, Vaughan, Grey: and so 'twill do
With some men else, that think themselves as safe
As thou and I, who (as thou know'st) are dear
To princely Richard and to Buckingham.
Catesby. The princes both make high account of you—
[*aside*] For they account his head upon the Bridge.

Hastings. I know they do, and I have well deserved it.

'Enter LORD STANLEY*'*

Come on, come on, where is your boar-spear, man?
Fear you the boar, and go so unprovided?
Stanley. My lord, good morrow; good morrow, Catesby:
You may jest on, but, by the holy rood,
I do not like these several councils, I.
Hastings. I hold my life as dear as you do yours;
And never in my days, I do protest,
Was it so precious to me as 'tis now:
Think you, but that I know our state secure,
I would be so triumphant as I am?
Stanley. The lords at Pomfret, when they rode from London,
Were jocund and supposed their states were sure,
And they indeed had no cause to mistrust;
But yet you see how soon the day o'ercast.
This sudden stab of rancour I misdoubt:
Pray God, I say, I prove a needless coward!
What, shall we toward the Tower? the day is spent.
Hastings. Come, come, have with you. Wot you what my lord?
To-day the lords you talked of are beheaded.
Stanley. They, for their truth, might better wear their heads
Than some that have accused them wear their hats.
But come, my lord, let's away.

'Enter a Pursuivant'

Hastings. Go on before; I'll talk with this good fellow. [*Stanley and Catesby depart*
How now, sirrah? how goes the world with thee?

Pursuivant. The better that your lordship please to ask.
Hastings. I tell thee, man, 'tis better with me now
Than when thou met'st me last where now we meet:
Then was I going prisoner to the Tower,
By the suggestion of the queen's allies;
But now, I tell thee (keep it to thyself)
This day those enemies are put to death,
And I in better state than e'er I was.
Pursuivant. God hold it, to your honour's good content!
Hastings. Gramercy, fellow: there, drink that for me. [*'throws him his purse'*
Pursuivant. I thank your honour. [*goes*

'Enter a Priest'

Priest. Well met, my lord; I am glad to see your honour.
Hastings. I thank thee, good Sir John, with all my heart.
I am in your debt for your last exercise;
Come the next Sabbath, and I will content you.
[*he whispers in his ear*

'Enter BUCKINGHAM*'*

Buckingham. What, talking with a priest, Lord Chamberlain?
Your friends at Pomfret, they do need the priest:
Your honour hath no shriving work in hand.
Hastings. Good faith, and when I met this holy man,
The men you talk of came into my mind.
What, go you toward the Tower?
Buckingham. I do, my lord; but long I cannot stay there:
I shall return before your lordship thence.

Hastings. Nay, like enough, for I stay dinner there.
(*Buckingham.* And supper too, although thou
know'st it not.
[*aloud*] Come, will you go?
Hastings. I'll wait upon your lordship.
[*they go off together*

[3. 3.] *Pomfret Castle*

'*Enter* SIR RICHARD RATCLIFFE, *with halberds, carrying the nobles*' RIVERS, GREY, *and* VAUGHAN '*to death*'

Rivers. Sir Richard Ratcliffe, let me tell thee this:
To-day shalt thou behold a subject die
For truth, for duty, and for loyalty.
Grey. God bless the prince from all the pack of you!
A knot you are of damnéd blood-suckers.
Vaughan. You live that shall cry woe for
this hereafter.
Ratcliffe. Dispatch; the limit of your lives is out.
Rivers. O Pomfret, Pomfret! O thou bloody prison,
Fatal and ominous to noble peers!
Within the guilty closure of thy walls
Richard the Second here was hacked to death;
And, for more slander to thy dismal seat,
We give to thee our guiltless blood to drink.
Grey. Now Margaret's curse is fall'n upon our heads,
When she exclaimed on Hastings, you, and I,
For standing by when Richard stabbed her son.
Rivers. Then cursed she Richard, then cursed
she Buckingham,
Then cursed she Hastings. O, remember, God,
To hear her prayer for them, as now for us!
And for my sister and her princely sons,

Be satisfied, dear God, with our true blood,
Which, as thou know'st, unjustly must be spilt.
Ratcliffe. Make haste; the hour of death is expiate.
Rivers. Come, Grey, come, Vaughan, let us here embrace:
Farewell, until we meet again in heaven.
[*they are led away*

[3. 4.] *A room in the Tower of London*

BUCKINGHAM, STANLEY, HASTINGS, the BISHOP OF ELY, RATCLIFFE, LOVEL, with others, at a table

Hastings. Now, noble peers, the cause why we are met
Is to determine of the coronation.
In God's name, speak! when is the royal day?
Buckingham. Is all things ready for the royal time?
Stanley. It is, and wants but nomination.
Ely. To-morrow then I judge a happy day.
Buckingham. Who knows the Lord Protector's mind herein?
Who is most inward with the noble duke?
Ely. Your grace, we think, should soonest know his mind.
Buckingham. We know each other's faces: for our hearts,
He knows no more of mine than I of yours;
Or I of his, my lord, than you of mine.
Lord Hastings, you and he are near in love.
Hastings. I thank his grace, I know he loves me well;
But, for his purpose in the coronation,
I have not sounded him, nor he delivered
His gracious pleasure any way therein:

But you, my honourable lords, may name the time;
And in the duke's behalf I'll give my voice,
Which, I presume, he'll take in gentle part.

'*Enter* GLOUCESTER'

Ely. In happy time, here comes the duke himself.
Gloucester. My noble lords and cousins all, good morrow.
I have been long a sleeper; but I trust
My absence doth neglect no great design,
Which by my presence might have been concluded.
Buckingham. Had you not come upon your cue, my lord,
William Lord Hastings had pronounced your part—
I mean, your voice for crowning of the king.
Gloucester. Than my Lord Hastings no man might be bolder;
His lordship knows me well, and loves me well.
My lord of Ely, when I was last in Holborn,
I saw good strawberries in your garden there:
I do beseech you send for some of them.
Ely. Marry, and will, my lord, with all my heart.
[*he goes*
Gloucester. Cousin of Buckingham, a word with you.
[*drawing him aside*
Catesby hath sounded Hastings in our business,
And finds the testy gentleman so hot,
That he will lose his head ere give consent
His master's child, as worshipfully he terms it,
Shall lose the royalty of England's throne.
Buckingham. Withdraw yourself a while, I'll go with you. [*they go out*
Stanley. We have not yet set down this day of triumph.

To-morrow, in my judgement, is too sudden;
For I myself am not so well provided
As else I would be, were the day prolonged.

The Bishop of Ely *returns*

Ely. Where is my Lord the Duke of Gloucester?
I have sent for these strawberries.
Hastings. His grace looks cheerfully and smooth this morning;
There's some conceit or other likes him well,
When that he bids good-morrow with such spirit.
I think there's ne'er a man in Christendom
Can lesser hide his love or hate than he;
For by his face straight shall you know his heart.
Stanley. What of his heart perceive you in his face
By any likelihood he showed to-day?
Hastings. Marry, that with no man here he is offended;
For, were he, he had shown it in his looks.

Gloucester *and* Buckingham *return; Gloucester with a wonderful sour countenance, knitting his brow and gnawing his lip*

Gloucester. I pray you all, tell me what they deserve
That do conspire my death with devilish plots
Of damnéd witchcraft, and that have prevailed
Upon my body with their hellish charms?
Hastings. The tender love I bear your grace, my lord,
Makes me most forward in this princely presence
To doom th'offenders: whosoe'er they be,
I say, my lord, they have deservéd death.
Gloucester. Then be your eyes the witness of their evil.

Look how I am bewitched; behold, mine arm
Is like a blasted sapling withered up:
And this is Edward's wife, that monstrous witch,
Consorted with that harlot, strumpet Shore,
That by their witchcraft thus have markéd me.

Hastings. If they have done this deed, my noble lord,—

Gloucester. If! thou protector of this damnéd strumpet,
Talk'st thou to me of 'ifs'? Thou art a traitor:
Off with his head! Now, by Saint Paul I swear,
I will not dine until I see the same.
Lovel and Ratcliffe, look that it be done:
The rest that love me, rise and follow me.
[*all leave but Hastings, Ratcliffe and Lovel*

Hastings. Woe, woe for England! not a whit for me;
For I, too fond, might have prevented this.
Stanley did dream the boar did raze our helms,
And I did scorn it, and disdain to fly:
Three times to-day my foot-cloth horse did stumble,
And started when he looked upon the Tower,
As loath to bear me to the slaughter-house.
O, now I need the priest that spake to me:
I now repent I told the pursuivant,
As too triumphing, how mine enemies
To-day at Pomfret bloodily were butchered,
And I myself secure in grace and favour.
O Margaret, Margaret, now thy heavy curse
Is lighted on poor Hastings' wretched head!

Ratcliffe. Come, come, dispatch; the duke would be at dinner:
Make a short shrift; he longs to see your head.

Hastings. O momentary grace of mortal men,
Which we more hunt for than the grace of God!
Who builds his hope in air of your good looks

Lives like a drunken sailor on a mast,
Ready with every nod to tumble down
Into the fatal bowels of the deep.

Lovel. Come, come, dispatch; 'tis bootless to exclaim.

Hastings. O bloody Richard! miserable England!
I prophesy the fearfull'st time to thee
That ever wretched age hath looked upon.
Come, lead me to the block; bear him my head.
They smile at me who shortly shall be dead.

[*he is led away*

[3. 5.] *The Tower-walls*

Enter GLOUCESTER *and* BUCKINGHAM, '*in rotten armour, marvellous ill-favoured*'

Gloucester. Come, cousin, canst thou quake, and change thy colour,
Murder thy breath in middle of a word,
And then again begin, and stop again,
As if thou wert distraught and mad with terror?

Buckingham. Tut, I can counterfeit the deep tragedian,
Speak and look back, and pry on every side,
Tremble and start at wagging of a straw,
Intending deep suspicion: ghastly looks
Are at my service, like enforcéd smiles;
And both are ready in their offices,
At any time, to grace my stratagems.
But what, is Catesby gone?

Gloucester. He is; and, see, he brings the mayor along.

'*Enter the Mayor and* CATESBY'

Buckingham. Lord Mayor,— [*he starts*

Gloucester. Look to the drawbridge there!
Buckingham. Hark! a drum.
Gloucester. Catesby, o'erlook the walls.
Buckingham. Lord Mayor, the reason we have sent—
Gloucester. Look back, defend thee, here are enemies!
Buckingham. God and our innocence defend and guard us!
Gloucester. Be patient, they are friends, Ratcliffe and Lovel.

'Enter LOVEL *and* RATCLIFFE, *with Hastings' head'*

Lovel. Here is the head of that ignoble traitor,
The dangerous and unsuspected Hastings.
Gloucester. So dear I loved the man, that I must weep.
I took him for the plainest harmless creature
That breathed upon the earth a Christian;
Made him my book, wherein my soul recorded
The history of all her secret thoughts.
So smooth he daubed his vice with show of virtue
That, his apparent open guilt omitted,
I mean his conversation with Shore's wife,
He lived from all attainder of suspects.
Buckingham. Well, well, he was the covert'st shelt'red traitor.
Would you imagine, or almost believe,
Were't not that, by great preservation,
We live to tell it, that the subtle traitor
This day had plotted, in the council-house
To murder me and my good Lord of Gloucester?
Mayor. Had he done so?
Gloucester. What! think you we are Turks or infidels?
Or that we would, against the form of law,

Proceed thus rashly in the villain's death,
But that the extreme peril of the case,
The peace of England and our persons' safety,
Enforced us to this execution?
Mayor. Now, fair befall you! he deserved his death;
And your good graces both have well proceeded,
To warn false traitors from the like attempts.
Buckingham. I never looked for better at his hands,
After he once fell in with Mistress Shore.
Yet had we not determined he should die,
Until your lordship came to see his end,
Which now the loving haste of these our friends,
Something against our meanings, have prevented:
Because, my lord, I would have had you hear
The traitor speak and timorously confess
The manner and the purpose of his treasons;
That you might well have signified the same
Unto the citizens, who haply may
Misconster us in him and wail his death.
Mayor. But, my good lord, your grace's words shall serve,
As well as I had seen and heard him speak:
And do not doubt, right noble princes both,
But I'll acquaint our duteous citizens
With all your just proceedings in this cause.
Gloucester. And to that end we wished your lordship here,
T'avoid the censures of the carping world.
Buckingham. Which since you come too late of our intent,
Yet witness what you hear we did intend:
And so, my good Lord Mayor, we bid farewell.
[*the Mayor takes leave*

Gloucester. Go, after, after, cousin Buckingham.
The mayor towards Guildhall hies him in all post:
There, at your meet'st advantage of the time,
Infer the bastardy of Edward's children:
Tell them how Edward put to death a citizen,
Only for saying he would make his son
Heir to the crown, meaning indeed his house,
Which, by the sign thereof, was termèd so.
Moreover, urge his hateful luxury
And bestial appetite in change of lust;
Which stretched unto their servants,
daughters, wives,
Even where his raging eye or savage heart
Without control listed to make a prey.
Nay, for a need, thus far come near my person:
Tell them, when that my mother went with child
Of that insatiate Edward, noble York
My princely father then had wars in France;
And, by true computation of the time,
Found that the issue was not his begot;
Which well appearèd in his lineaments,
Being nothing like the noble duke my father:
Yet touch this sparingly, as 'twere far off,
Because, my lord, you know my mother lives.
Buckingham. Doubt not, my lord, I'll play the orator
As if the golden fee for which I plead
Were for myself: and so, my lord, adieu.
Gloucester. If you thrive well, bring them to
Baynard's Castle,
Where you shall find me well accompanied
With reverend fathers and well-learnèd bishops.
Buckingham. I go, and towards three or four o'clock
Look for the news that the Guildhall affords. [*goes*
Gloucester. Go, Lovel, with all speed to Doctor Shaw;

[*To Catesby*] Go thou to Friar Penker; bid them both
Meet me within this hour at Baynard's Castle.
[*they depart*
Now will I go to take some privy order
To draw the brats of Clarence out of sight;
And to give notice that no manner person
Have any time recourse unto the princes. [*he goes*

[3.6.] *London. A street*

'*Enter a Scrivener*', *with a paper in his hand*

Scrivener. Here is the indictment of the good
Lord Hastings,
Which in a set hand fairly is engrossed,
That it may be to-day read o'er in Paul's.
And mark how well the sequel hangs together:
Eleven hours I have spent to write it over,
For yesternight by Catesby was it sent me;
The precedent was full as long a-doing:
And yet within these five hours Hastings lived,
Untainted, unexamined, free, at liberty.
Here's a good world the while! Who is so gross,
That cannot see this palpable device?
Yet who's so bold, but says he sees it not?
Bad is the world; and all will come to nought,
When such ill dealing must be seen in thought.
[*he goes*

[3. 7.] *A court-yard before Baynard's Castle*

Enter GLOUCESTER *and* BUCKINGHAM *at different doors*

Gloucester. How now, how now, what say the citizens?
Buckingham. Now, by the holy mother of our Lord,
The citizens are mum, say not a word.
Gloucester. Touched you the bastardy of Edward's children?
Buckingham. I did; with his contract with Lady Lucy,
And his contract by deputy in France;
Th'insatiate greediness of his desire,
And his enforcement of the city wives;
His tyranny for trifles; his own bastardy,
As being got, your father then in France,
And his resemblance, being not like the duke:
Withal I did infer your lineaments,
Being the right idea of your father,
Both in your form and nobleness of mind;
Laid open all your victories in Scotland,
Your discipline in war, wisdom in peace,
Your bounty, virtue, fair humility;
Indeed left nothing fitting for your purpose
Untouched or slightly handled in discourse:
And when mine oratory drew toward end,
I bid them that did love their country's good
Cry 'God save Richard, England's royal king!'
Gloucester. And did they so?
Buckingham. No, so God help me, they spake not a word;
But, like dumb statuas or breathing stones,

Stared each on other, and looked deadly pale.
Which when I saw, I reprehended them,
And asked the Mayor what meant this wilful silence:
His answer was, the people were not uséd
To be spoke to but by the Recorder.
Then he was urged to tell my tale again:
'Thus saith the duke, thus hath the duke inferred';
But nothing spoke in warrant from himself.
When he had done, some followers of mine own
At lower end of the hall hurled up their caps,
And some ten voices cried 'God save King Richard!'
And thus I took the vantage of those few,
'Thanks, gentle citizens and friends'! quoth I,
'This general applause and cheerful shout
Argues your wisdoms and your love to Richard'—
And even here brake off and came away.

Gloucester. What tongueless blocks were they! would they not speak?

Buckingham. No, by my troth, my lord.

Gloucester. Will not the Mayor then and his brethren come?

Buckingham. The Mayor is here at hand: intend some fear;
Be not you spoke with, but by mighty suit:
And look you get a prayer-book in your hand,
And stand between two churchmen, good my lord;
For on that ground I'll make a holy descant:
And be not easily won to our requests;
Play the maid's part, still answer nay, and take it.

Gloucester. I go; and if you plead as well for them
As I can say nay to thee for myself,
No doubt we'll bring it to a happy issue.

Buckingham. Go, go up to the leads; the Lord Mayor knocks. [*Gloucester hurries away*

The Mayor and Citizens enter the court-yard

Welcome, my lord: I dance attendance here;
I think the duke will not be spoke withal.

CATESBY comes forth

Catesby, what says your lord to my request?
Catesby. He doth entreat your grace, my noble lord,
To visit him to-morrow or next day:
He is within, with two right reverend fathers,
Divinely bent to meditation;
And in no worldly suits would he be moved,
To draw him from his holy exercise.
Buckingham. Return, good Catesby, to the gracious duke:
Tell him, myself, the Mayor, and Alderman,
In deep designs, in matter of great moment,
No less importing than our general good,
Are come to have some conference with his grace.
Catesby. I'll signify so much unto him straight. [*goes in*
Buckingham. Ah, ha, my lord, this prince is not an Edward!
He is not lolling on a lewd love-bed,
But on his knees at meditation;
Not dallying with a brace of courtezans,
But meditating with two deep divines;
Not sleeping, to engross his idle body,
But praying, to enrich his watchful soul:
Happy were England, would this virtuous prince
Take on his grace the sovereignty thereof:
But, sure, I fear, we shall not win him to it.
Mayor. Marry, God defend his grace should say us nay!

Buckingham. I fear he will. Here Catesby comes again.

Catesby returns

Now, Catesby, what says his grace?
Catesby. He wonders to what end you have assembled
Such troops of citizens to come to him,
His grace not being warned thereof before:
He fears, my lord, you mean no good to him.
Buckingham. Sorry I am my noble cousin should
Suspect me that I mean no good to him:
By heaven, we come to him in perfit love;
And so once more return and tell his grace.
[*Catesby goes in again*
When holy and devout religious men
Are at their beads, 'tis much to draw them thence,
So sweet is zealous contemplation.

Gloucester appears 'aloft, between two Bishops'; Catesby returns

Mayor. See, where his grace stands, 'tween two clergymen!
Buckingham. Two props of virtue for a Christian prince,
To stay him from the fall of vanity:
And, see, a book of prayer in his hand,
True ornaments to know a holy man.
Famous Plantagenet, most gracious prince,
Lend favourable ear to our requests;
And pardon us the interruption
Of thy devotion and right Christian zeal.
Gloucester. My lord, there needs no such apology:
I do beseech your grace to pardon me,

Who, earnest in the service of my God,
Deferred the visitation of my friends.
But, leaving this, what is your grace's pleasure?
Buckingham. Even that, I hope, which pleaseth God above
And all good men of this ungoverned isle.
Gloucester. I do suspect I have done some offence
That seems disgracious in the city's eye,
And that you come to reprehend my ignorance.
Buckingham. You have, my lord: would it might please your grace,
On our entreaties, to amend your fault!
Gloucester. Else wherefore breathe I in a Christian land?
Buckingham. Know then, it is your fault that you resign
The supreme seat, the throne majestical,
The scept'red office of your ancestors,
Your state of fortune and your due of birth,
The lineal glory of your royal house,
To the corruption of a blemished stock:
Whiles, in the mildness of your sleepy thoughts,
Which here we waken to our country's good,
The noble isle doth want her proper limbs;
Her face defaced with scars of infamy,
Her royal stock graffed with ignoble plants,
And almost should'red in the swallowing gulf
Of dark forgetfulness and deep oblivion.
Which to recure, we heartily solicit
Your gracious self to take on you the charge
And kingly government of this your land;
Not as protector, steward, substitute,
Or lowly factor for another's gain;
But as successively, from blood to blood,

Your right of birth, your empery, your own.
For this, consorted with the citizens,
Your very worshipful and loving friends,
And by their vehement instigation,
In this just cause come I to move your grace.
Gloucester. I cannot tell if to depart in silence
Or bitterly to speak in your reproof
Best fitteth my degree or your condition:
If not to answer, you might haply think
Tongue-tied ambition, not replying, yielded
To bear the golden yoke of sovereignty,
Which fondly you would here impose on me;
If to reprove you for this suit of yours,
So seasoned with your faithful love to me,
Then, on the other side, I checked my friends.
Therefore—to speak, and to avoid the first,
And then, in speaking, not to incur the last—
Definitively thus I answer you:
Your love deserves my thanks, but my desert
Unmeritable shuns your high request.
First, if all obstacles were cut away
And that my path were even to the crown,
As the ripe revenue and due of birth,
Yet so much is my poverty of spirit,
So mighty and so many my defects,
That I would rather hide me from my greatness,
Being a bark to brook no mighty sea,
Than in my greatness covet to be hid
And in the vapour of my glory smothered.
But, God be thanked, there is no need of me,
And much I need to help you, were there need:
The royal tree hath left us royal fruit,
Which, mellowed by the stealing hours of time,
Will well become the seat of majesty,

And make, no doubt, us happy by his reign.
On him I lay that you would lay on me,
The right and fortune of his happy stars,
Which God defend that I should wring from him!

Buckingham. My lord, this argues conscience in your grace;
But the respects thereof are nice and trivial,
All circumstances well consideréd.
You say that Edward is your brother's son:
So say we too, but not by Edward's wife;
For first was he contract to Lady Lucy—
Your mother lives a witness to his vow—
And afterward by substitute betrothed
To Bona, sister to the King of France.
These both put off, a poor petitioner,
A care-crazed mother to a many sons,
A beauty-waning and distresséd widow,
Even in the afternoon of her best days,
Made prize and purchase of his wanton eye,
Seduced the pitch and height of his degree
To base declension and loathed bigamy:
By her, in his unlawful bed, he got
This Edward, whom our manners call the prince.
More bitterly could I expostulate,
Save that, for reverence to some alive,
I give a sparing limit to my tongue.
Then, good my lord, take to your royal self
This proffered benefit of dignity;
If not to bless us and the land withal,
Yet to draw forth your noble ancestry
From the corruption of abusing times
Unto a lineal true-derivéd course.

Mayor. Do, good my lord, your citizens entreat you.

Buckingham. Refuse not, mighty lord, this proffered love.
Catesby. O, make them joyful, grant their lawful suit!
Gloucester. Alas, why would you heap this care on me?
I am unfit for state and majesty:
I do beseech you, take it not amiss;
I cannot nor I will not yield to you.
Buckingham. If you refuse it—as, in love and zeal,
Loath to depose the child, your brother's son;
As well we know your tenderness of heart
And gentle, kind, effeminate remorse,
Which we have noted in you to your kindred,
And egally indeed to all estates—
Yet know, whe'er you accept our suit or no,
Your brother's son shall never reign our king;
But we will plant some other in the throne,
To the disgrace and downfall of your house:
And in this resolution here we leave you.
Come, citizens. Zounds! I'll entreat no more.
Gloucester. O, do not swear, my lord of Buckingham.
[*Buckingham stalks out; citizens slowly follow*
Catesby. Call him again, sweet prince, accept their suit:
If you deny them, all the land will rue it.
Gloucester. Will you enforce me to a world of cares?
Call them again: I am not made of stone,
But penetrable to your kind entreaties,
Albeit against my conscience and my soul.

'BUCKINGHAM and the rest' return

Cousin of Buckingham, and sage grave men,
Since you will buckle fortune on my back,

To bear her burthen, whe'er I will or no,
I must have patience to endure the load:
But if black scandal or foul-faced reproach
Attend the sequel of your imposition,
Your mere enforcement shall acquittance me
From all the impure blots and stains thereof;
For God doth know, and you may partly see,
How far I am from the desire of this.

Mayor. God bless your grace! we see it, and will say it.

Gloucester. In saying so, you shall but say the truth.

Buckingham. Then I salute you with this royal title:
Long live King Richard, England's worthy king!

All. Amen.

Buckingham. To-morrow may it please you to be crowned?

Gloucester. Even when you please, for you will have it so.

Buckingham. To-morrow then we will attend your grace:
And so most joyfully we take our leave.

Gloucester. Come, let us to our holy work again.
Farewell, my cousin; farewell, gentle friends.

[*they go*

[4. 1.] *Before the Tower*

Enter QUEEN ELIZABETH, DUCHESS OF YORK, *and* MARQUIS OF DORSET; *meeting* ANNE, DUCHESS OF GLOUCESTER, *and* LADY MARGARET PLANTAGENET, CLARENCE'S *young daughter*

Duchess. Who meets us here? my niece Plantagenet,
Led in the hand of her kind aunt of Gloucester?
Now, for my life, she's wand'ring to the Tower,
On pure heart's love to greet the tender princes.
Daughter, well met.
Anne. God give your graces both
A happy and a joyful time of day!
Queen Elizabeth. As much to you, good sister!
Whither away?
Anne. No farther than the Tower, and, as I guess,
Upon the like devotion as yourselves,
To gratulate the gentle princes there.
Queen Elizabeth. Kind sister, thanks: we'll enter all together.

BRAKENBURY *comes from the Tower*

And, in good time, here the lieutenant comes.
Master Lieutenant, pray you, by your leave,
How doth the prince, and my young son of York?
Brakenbury. Right well, dear madam. By your patience,
I may not suffer you to visit them;
The king hath strictly charged the contrary.
Queen Elizabeth. The king! who's that?
Brakenbury. I mean the Lord Protector.
Queen Elizabeth. The Lord protect him from that kingly title!

Hath he set bounds between their love and me?
I am their mother; who shall bar me from them?
Duchess. I am their father's mother; I will see them.
Anne. Their aunt I am in law, in love their mother:
Then bring me to their sights; I'll bear thy blame,
And take thy office from thee, on my peril.
Brakenbury. No, madam, no; I may not leave it so:
I am bound by oath, and therefore pardon me.
[*he goes within*

LORD STANLEY comes up

Stanley. Let me but meet you, ladies, one hour hence,
And I'll salute your grace of York as mother,
And reverend looker-on, of two fair queens.
[*to Anne*] Come, madam, you must straight to Westminster,
There to be crownéd Richard's royal queen.
Queen Elizabeth. Ah, cut my lace asunder,
That my pent heart may have some scope to beat,
Or else I swoon with this dead-killing news!
Anne. Despiteful tidings! O unpleasing news!
Dorset. Be of good cheer: mother, how fares your grace?
Queen Elizabeth. O Dorset, speak not to me, get thee gone!
Death and destruction dogs thee at thy heels;
Thy mother's name is ominous to children.
If thou wilt outstrip death, go cross the seas,
And live with Richmond, from the reach of hell:
Go, hie thee, hie thee from this slaughter-house,
Lest thou increase the number of the dead;
And make me die the thrall of Margaret's curse,
Nor mother, wife, nor England's counted queen.

Stanley. Full of wise care is this your counsel, madam.
[*to Dorset*] Take all the swift advantage of the hours;
You shall have letters from me to my son
In your behalf, to meet you on the way:
Be not ta'en tardy by unwise delay.
Duchess. O ill-dispersing wind of misery!
O my accurséd womb, the bed of death!
A cockatrice hast thou hatched to the world,
Whose unavoided eye is murderous.
Stanley. Come, madam, come; I in all haste was sent.
Anne. And I with all unwillingness will go.
O, would to God that the inclusive verge
Of golden metal that must round my brow
Were red-hot steel, to sear me to the brains!
Anointed let me be with deadly venom,
And die ere men can say, 'God save the queen!'
Queen Elizabeth. Go, go, poor soul, I envy not thy glory:
To feed my humour, wish thyself no harm.
Anne. No? Why, when he that is my husband now
Came to me, as I followed Henry's corse,
When scarce the blood was well washed from his hands
Which issued from my other angel husband,
And that dear saint which then I weeping followed—
O, when, I say, I looked on Richard's face,
This was my wish: 'Be thou', quoth I, 'accursed,
For making me, so young, so old a widow!
And, when thou wed'st, let sorrow haunt thy bed;
And be thy wife—if any be so—made
More miserable by the life of thee
Than thou hast made me by my dear lord's death!'
Lo, ere I can repeat this curse again,

Within so small a time, my woman's heart
Grossly grew captive to his honey words
And proved the subject of mine own soul's curse,
Which hitherto hath held mine eyes from rest;
For never yet one hour in his bed
Did I enjoy the golden dew of sleep,
But with his timorous dreams was still awaked.
Besides, he hates me for my father Warwick;
And will, no doubt, shortly be rid of me.

Queen Elizabeth. Poor heart, adieu! I pity thy complaining.

Anne. No more than with my soul I mourn for yours.

Queen Elizabeth. Farewell, thou woeful welcomer of glory!

Anne. Adieu, poor soul, that tak'st thy leave of it!

Duchess. [*to Dorset*] Go thou to Richmond, and good fortune guide thee!
[*to Anne*] Go thou to Richard, and good angels tend thee!
[*to Queen Elizabeth*] Go thou to sanctuary, and good thoughts possess thee!
I to my grave, where peace and rest lie with me!
Eighty odd years of sorrow have I seen,
And each hour's joy wracked with a week of teen.

Queen Elizabeth. Stay, yet look back with me unto the Tower.
Pity, you ancient stones, those tender babes
Whom envy hath immured within your walls!
Rough cradle for such little pretty ones!
Rude ragged nurse, old sullen playfellow
For tender princes, use my babies well!
So foolish sorrow bids your stones farewell.

[*they depart*

[4. 2.] *London. The Palace*

'Sennet. Enter RICHARD, *in pomp', crowned;* BUCKINGHAM, CATESBY, *a Page, and others*

King Richard. Stand all apart. Cousin of Buckingham!
Buckingham. My gracious sovereign!
King Richard. Give me thy hand. [*trumpets sound as he ascends the throne.*] Thus high, by thy advice,
And thy assistance, is King Richard seated:
But shall we wear these glories for a day?
Or shall they last, and we rejoice in them?
Buckingham. Still live they and for ever let them last!
King Richard. Ah Buckingham, now do I play the touch,
To try if thou be current gold indeed:
Young Edward lives; think now what I would speak.
Buckingham. Say on, my loving lord.
King Richard. Why, Buckingham, I say I would be king.
Buckingham. Why, so you are, my thrice-renownéd lord.
King Richard. Ha? am I king? 'tis so—but Edward lives.
Buckingham. True, noble prince.
King Richard. O bitter consequence!
That Edward still should live 'true noble prince'!
Cousin, thou wast not wont to be so dull.
Shall I be plain? I wish the bastards dead,
And I would have it suddenly performed.
What say'st thou now? speak suddenly, be brief.

Buckingham. Your grace may do your pleasure.
King Richard. Tut, tut, thou art all ice, thy kindness freezes:
Say, have I thy consent that they shall die?
Buckingham. Give me some little breath, some pause, dear lord,
Before I positively speak in this:
I will resolve you herein presently. [*he goes*
(*Catesby.* The king is angry: see, he gnaws his lip.
King Richard. I will converse with iron-witted fools
And unrespective boys: none are for me [*descends from*
That look into me with considerate eyes: *his throne*
High-reaching Buckingham grows circumspect.
Boy!
Page. My lord?
King Richard. Know'st thou not any whom corrupting gold
Will tempt unto a close exploit of death?
Page. I know a discontented gentleman
Whose humble means match not his haughty spirit:
Gold were as good as twenty orators,
And will, no doubt, tempt him to any thing.
King Richard. What is his name?
Page. His name, my lord, is Tyrrel.
King Richard. I partly know the man: go, call him hither, boy [*Page goes*
The deep-revolving witty Buckingham
No more shall be the neighbour to my counsels.
Hath he so long held out with me untired,
And stops he now for breath? Well, be it so.

'*Enter* STANLEY'

How now, Lord Stanley!
Stanley. Know, my loving lord,

The Marquis Dorset, as I hear, is fled
To Richmond in the parts where he abides.
[*stands apart*

King Richard. Come hither, Catesby. Rumour it abroad
That Anne, my wife, is very grievous sick:
I will take order for her keeping close.
Inquire me out some mean poor gentleman,
Whom I will marry straight to Clarence' daughter:
The boy is foolish, and I fear not him.
Look, how thou dream'st! I say again, give out
That Anne, my queen, is sick and like to die.
About it! for it stands me much upon
To stop all hopes whose growth may damage me.
[*Catesby hurries forth*
I must be married to my brother's daughter,
Or else my kingdom stands on brittle glass...
Murder her brothers, and then marry her!
Uncertain way of gain! But I am in
So far in blood that sin will pluck on sin:
Tear-falling pity dwells not in this eye.

Re-enter Page with TYRREL

Is thy name Tyrrel?

Tyrrel. James Tyrrel, and your most obedient subject.

King Richard. Art thou, indeed?

Tyrrel. Prove me, my gracious lord.

King Richard. Dar'st thou resolve to kill a friend of mine?

Tyrrel. Please you, I had rather kill two enemies.

King Richard. Why, there thou hast it: two deep enemies,
Foes to my rest and my sweet sleep's disturbers,
Are they that I would have thee deal upon:

Tyrrel, I mean those bastards in the Tower.
Tyrrel. Let me have open means to come to them,
And soon I'll rid you from the fear of them.
King Richard. Thou sing'st sweet music. Hark, come hither, Tyrrel:
Go, by this token: rise, and lend thine ear: [*'whispers'*
There is no more but so: say it is done,
And I will love thee, and prefer thee for it.
Tyrrel. I will dispatch it straight. [*goes*

BUCKINGHAM returns

Buckingham. My lord, I have considered in my mind
The late request that you did sound me in.
King Richard. Well, let that rest. Dorset is fled to Richmond.
Buckingham. I hear the news, my lord.
King Richard. Stanley, he is your wife's son: look unto it.
Buckingham. My lord, I claim the gift, my due by promise,
For which your honour and your faith is pawned—
Th'earldom of Hereford and the movables
Which you have promiséd I shall possess.
King Richard. Stanley, look to your wife: if she convey
Letters to Richmond, you shall answer it.
Buckingham. What says your highness to my just request?
King Richard. I do remember me, Henry the Sixth
Did prophesy that Richmond should be king,
When Richmond was a little peevish boy.
A king! perhaps—

Buckingham. My lord!
King Richard. How chance the prophet could not at that time
Have told me, I being by, that I should kill him?
Buckingham. My lord, your promise for the earldom—
King Richard. Richmond! When last I was at Exeter,
The mayor in courtesy showed me the castle,
And called it Rougemont: at which name I started,
Because a bard of Ireland told me once
I should not live long after I saw Richmond.
Buckingham. My lord!
King Richard. Ay, what's o'clock?
Buckingham. I am thus bold to put your grace in mind
Of what you promised me.
King Richard. Well, but what's o'clock?
Buckingham. Upon the stroke of ten.
King Richard. Well, let it strike.
Buckingham. Why let it strike?
King Richard. Because that, like a Jack, thou keep'st the stroke
Betwixt thy begging and my meditation.
I am not in the giving vein to-day.
Buckingham. May it please you to resolve me in my suit?
King Richard. Thou troublest me, I am not in the vein. [*goes*
Buckingham. And is it thus? repays he my deep service
With such contempt? made I him king for this?
O, let me think on Hastings, and be gone
To Brecknock, while my fearful head is on! [*goes*

[4. 3.] *The same, later*

'Enter TYRREL*'*

Tyrrel. The tyrannous and bloody act is done,
The most arch deed of piteous massacre
That ever yet this land was guilty of.
Dighton and Forrest, whom I did suborn
To do this piece of ruthless butchery,
Albeit they were fleshed villains, bloody dogs,
Melting with tenderness and mild compassion,
Wept like two children in their death's sad story.
'O, thus,' quoth Dighton, 'lay the gentle babes':
'Thus, thus,' quoth Forrest, 'girdling one another
Within their alabaster innocent arms:
Their lips were four red roses on a stalk,
Which in their summer beauty kissed each other.
A book of prayers on their pillow lay;
Which once,' quoth Forrest, 'almost changed my mind;
But O! the devil'—there the villain stopped;
Whilst Dighton thus told on: 'We smotheréd
The most replenishéd sweet work of Nature
That from the prime creation e'er she framed.'
Hence all o'er gone with conscience and remorse,
They could not speak; and so I left them both,
To bear this tidings to the bloody king.
And here he comes.

Enter KING RICHARD

All health, my sovereign lord!
King Richard. Kind Tyrrel, am I happy in thy news?
Tyrrel. If to have done the thing you gave in charge
Beget your happiness, be happy then,
For it is done.

King Richard. But didst thou see them dead?
Tyrrel. I did, my lord.
King Richard. And buried, gentle Tyrrel?
Tyrrel. The chaplain of the Tower hath buried them;
But where, to say the truth, I do not know.
King Richard. Come to me, Tyrrel, soon at after-supper,
When thou shalt tell the process of their death.
Meantime, but think how I may do thee good,
And be inheritor of thy desire.
Farewell till then.
Tyrrel. I humbly take my leave. [*he goes*
King Richard. The son of Clarence have I pent up close;
His daughter meanly have I matched in marriage;
The sons of Edward sleep in Abraham's bosom,
And Anne my wife hath bid this world good night.
Now, for I know the Breton Richmond aims
At young Elizabeth, my brother's daughter,
And, by that knot, looks proudly on the crown,
To her go I, a jolly thriving wooer.

'*Enter* RATCLIFFE'

Ratcliffe. My lord!
King Richard. Good or bad news, that thou com'st in so bluntly?
Ratcliffe. Bad news, my lord: Morton is fled to Richmond;
And Buckingham, backed with the hardy Welshmen,
Is in the field, and still his power increaseth.
King Richard. Ely with Richmond troubles me more near
Than Buckingham and his rash-levied strength.

Come, I have learned that fearful commenting
Is leaden servitor to dull delay;
Delay leads impotent and snail-paced beggary:
Then fiery expedition be my wing,
Jove's Mercury, and herald for a king!
Go, muster men: my counsel is my shield;
We must be brief when traitors brave the field.
[*they go*

[4. 4.] *Before the palace*

'*Enter old* QUEEN MARGARET'

Queen Margaret. So now prosperity begins to mellow
And drop into the rotten mouth of death.
Here in these confines slily have I lurked,
To watch the waning of mine enemies.
A dire induction am I witness to,
And will to France, hoping the consequence
Will prove as bitter, black, and tragical.
Withdraw thee, wretched Margaret: who comes here?

Enter QUEEN ELIZABETH *and the* DUCHESS OF YORK

Queen Elizabeth. Ah, my poor princes! ah, my tender babes!
My unblown flowers, new-appearing sweets!
If yet your gentle souls fly in the air
And be not fixed in doom perpetual,
Hover about me with your airy wings
And hear your mother's lamentation!
(*Queen Margaret.* Hover about her; say, that right for right
Hath dimmed your infant morn to agéd night.
Duchess. So many miseries have crazed my voice,

That my woe-wearied tongue is still and mute.
Edward Plantagenet, why art thou dead?
(*Queen Margaret.* Plantagenet doth quit Plantagenet,
Edward for Edward pays a dying debt.
Queen Elizabeth. Wilt thou, O God, fly from such gentle lambs,
And throw them in the entrails of the wolf?
When didst thou sleep when such a deed was done?
(*Queen Margaret.* When holy Harry died, and my sweet son.
Duchess. Dead life, blind sight, poor mortal living ghost,
Woe's scene, world's shame, grave's due by life usurped,
Brief abstract and record of tedious days,
Rest thy unrest on England's lawful earth,
Unlawfully made drunk with innocent blood!
[*sits*
Queen Elizabeth. Ah, that thou wouldst as soon afford a grave
As thou canst yield a melancholy seat!
Then would I hide my bones, not rest them here.
Ah, who hath any cause to mourn but we?
[*sits down by her*
Queen Margaret. [*advancing*] If ancient sorrow be most reverend,
Give mine the benefit of seniory,
And let my griefs frown on the upper hand.
If sorrow can admit society, [*sits down with them*
Tell o'er your woes again by viewing mine:
I had an Edward, till a Richard killed him;
I had a Harry, till a Richard killed him:
Thou hadst an Edward, till a Richard killed him;
Thou hadst a Richard, till a Richard killed him.

Duchess. I had a Richard too, and thou didst kill him;
I had a Rutland too, thou holp'st to kill him.
Queen Margaret. Thou hadst a Clarence too, and Richard killed him.
From forth the kennel of thy womb hath crept
A hell-hound that doth hunt us all to death:
That dog, that had his teeth before his eyes,
To worry lambs and lap their gentle blood;
That foul defacer of God's handiwork;
That excellent grand tyrant of the earth,
That reigns in gallèd eyes of weeping souls—
Thy womb let loose, to chase us to our graves.
O upright, just, and true-disposing God,
How do I thank thee, that this carnal cur
Preys on the issue of his mother's body,
And makes her pew-fellow with others' moan!
Duchess. O Harry's wife, triumph not in my woes!
God witness with me, I have wept for thine.
Queen Margaret. Bear with me; I am hungry for revenge,
And now I cloy me with beholding it.
Thy Edward he is dead, that killed my Edward;
Thy other Edward dead, to quit my Edward;
Young York he is but boot, because both they
Matched not the high perfection of my loss:
Thy Clarence he is dead that stabbed my Edward;
And the beholders of this frantic play,
Th'adulterate Hastings, Rivers, Vaughan, Grey,
Untimely smothered in their dusky graves.
Richard yet lives, hell's black intelligencer,
Only reserved their factor, to buy souls
And send them thither: but at hand, at hand,
Ensues his piteous and unpitied end:

Earth gapes, hell burns, fiends roar, saints pray,
To have him suddenly conveyed from hence:
Cancel his bond of life, dear God, I plead,
That I may live and say 'The dog is dead!'

Queen Elizabeth. O, thou didst prophesy the time would come
That I should wish for thee to help me curse
That bottled spider, that foul bunch-backed toad!

Queen Margaret. I called thee then vain flourish of my fortune;
I called thee then poor shadow, painted queen,
The presentation of but what I was;
The flattering index of a direful pageant;
One heaved a-high, to be hurled down below;
A mother only mocked with two fair babes;
A dream of what thou wast, a garish flag,
To be the aim of every dangerous shot;
A sign of dignity, a breath, a bubble;
A queen in jest, only to fill the scene.
Where is thy husband now? where be thy brothers?
Where be thy two sons? wherein dost thou joy?
Who sues, and kneels and says, 'God save the queen'?
Where be the bending peers that flatteréd thee?
Where be the thronging troops that followéd thee?
Decline all this, and see what now thou art:
For happy wife, a most distresséd widow;
For joyful mother, one that wails the name;
For queen, a very caitiff crowned with care;
For one being sued to, one that humbly sues;
For she that scorned at me, now scorned of me;
For she being feared of all, now fearing one;
For she commanding all, obeyed of none.
Thus hath the course of Justice whirled about,
And left thee but a very prey to time;

Having no more but thought of what thou wast,
To torture thee the more, being what thou art.
Thou didst usurp my place, and dost thou not
Usurp the just proportion of my sorrow?
Now thy proud neck bears half my burthened yoke;
From which even here I slip my weary head,
And leave the burthen of it all—on thee.
Farewell, York's wife, and queen of sad mischance:
These English woes shall make me smile in France.

Queen Elizabeth. O thou well skilled in curses, stay awhile,
And teach me how to curse mine enemies!

Queen Margaret. Forbear to sleep the nights, and fast the days;
Compare dead happiness with living woe;
Think that thy babes were sweeter than they were,
And he that slew them fouler than he is:
Bett'ring thy loss makes the bad causer worse:
Revolving this will teach thee how to curse.

Queen Elizabeth. My words are dull; O, quicken them with thine!

Queen Margaret. Thy woes will make them sharp and pierce like mine. [*she goes*

Duchess. Why should calamity be full of words?

Queen Elizabeth. Windy attorneys to their client woes,
Airy succeeders of intestate joys,
Poor breathing orators of miseries!
Let them have scope: though what they will impart
Help nothing else, yet do they ease the heart.

Duchess. If so, then be not tongue-tied: go with me,
And in the breath of bitter words let's smother
My damnèd son, that thy two sweet sons smothered.
The trumpet sounds: be copious in exclaims.

'Enter KING RICHARD *and his train', marching with drums and trumpets*

King Richard. Who intercepts me in my expedition?
Duchess. O, she that might have intercepted thee,
By strangling thee in her accurséd womb,
From all the slaughters, wretch, that thou hast done!
Queen Elizabeth. Hid'st thou that forehead with a golden crown,
Where should be branded, if that right were right,
The slaughter of the prince that owed that crown,
And the dire death of my poor sons and brothers?
Tell me, thou villain slave, where are my children?
Duchess. Thou toad, thou toad, where is thy brother Clarence?
And little Ned Plantagenet, his son?
Queen Elizabeth. Where is the gentle Rivers, Vaughan, Grey?
Duchess. Where is kind Hastings?
King Richard. A flourish, trumpets! strike alarum, drums!
Let not the heavens hear these tell-tale women
Rail on the Lord's anointed: strike, I say!
['*Flourish. Alarums*'
Either be patient, and entreat me fair,
Or with the clamorous report of war
Thus will I drown your exclamations.
Duchess. Art thou my son?
King Richard. Ay, I thank God, my father, and yourself.
Duchess. Then patiently hear my impatience.
King Richard. Madam, I have a touch of your condition,
That cannot brook the accent of reproof.

Duchess. O, let me speak!
King Richard. Do then; but I'll not hear.
Duchess. I will be mild and gentle in my words.
King Richard. And brief, good mother, for I am in haste.
Duchess. Art thou so hasty? I have stayed for thee,
God knows, in torment and in agony.
King Richard. And came I not at last to comfort you?
Duchess. No, by the holy rood, thou know'st it well,
Thou cam'st on earth to make the earth my hell.
A grievous burthen was thy birth to me;
Tetchy and wayward was thy infancy;
Thy school-days frightful, desp'rate, wild, and furious;
Thy prime of manhood daring, bold, and venturous;
Thy age confirmed, proud, subtle, sly and bloody,
More mild but yet more harmful-kind in hatred.
What comfortable hour canst thou name,
That ever graced me with thy company?
King Richard. Faith, none, but Humphrey Hour, that called your grace
To breakfast once forth of my company.
If I be so disgracious in your eye,
Let me march on, and not offend you, madam.
Strike up the drum.
Duchess. I prithee, hear me speak.
King Richard. You speak too bitterly.
Duchess. Hear me a word;
For I shall never speak to thee again.
King Richard. So.
Duchess. Either thou wilt die, by God's just ordinance,
Ere from this war thou turn a conqueror,
Or I with grief and extreme age shall perish
And never more behold thy face again.

Therefore take with thee my most grievous curse,
Which, in the day of battle, tire thee more
Than all the complete armour that thou wear'st!
My prayers on the adverse party fight;
And there the little souls of Edward's children
Whisper the spirits of thine enemies
And promise them success and victory.
Bloody thou art, bloody will be thy end;
Shame serves thy life and doth thy death attend.
[*she goes*

Queen Elizabeth. Though far more cause, yet much less spirit to curse
Abides in me; I say amen to her.

King Richard. Stay, madam; I must talk a word with you. [*draws her aside*

Queen Elizabeth. I have no moe sons of the royal blood
For thee to slaughter: for my daughters, Richard,
They shall be praying nuns, not weeping queens;
And therefore level not to hit their lives.

King Richard. You have a daughter called Elizabeth,
Virtuous and fair, royal and gracious.

Queen Elizabeth. And must she die for this? O, let her live,
And I'll corrupt her manners, stain her beauty,
Slander myself as false to Edward's bed,
Throw over her the veil of infamy:
So she may live unscarred of bleeding slaughter,
I will confess she was not Edward's daughter.

King Richard. Wrong not her birth, she is a royal princess.

Queen Elizabeth. To save her life, I'll say she is not so.

King Richard. Her life is safest only in her birth.

Queen Elizabeth. And only in that safety died her brothers.
King Richard. No, at their births good stars were opposite.
Queen Elizabeth. No, to their lives ill friends were contrary.
King Richard. All unavoided is the doom of destiny.
Queen Elizabeth. True, when avoided grace makes destiny:
My babes were destined to a fairer death,
If grace had blessed thee with a fairer life.
King Richard. You speak as if that I had slain my cousins!
Queen Elizabeth. Cousins indeed, and by their uncle cozened
Of comfort, kingdom, kindred, freedom, life.
Whose hand soever lanced their tender hearts,
Thy head, all indirectly, gave direction:
No doubt the murd'rous knife was dull and blunt
Till it was whetted on thy stone-hard heart
To revel in the entrails of my lambs.
But that still use of grief makes wild grief tame,
My tongue should to thy ears not name my boys
Till that my nails were anchored in thine eyes;
And I, in such a desp'rate bay of death,
Like a poor bark, of sails and tackling reft,
Rush all to pieces on thy rocky bosom.
King Richard. Madam, so thrive I in my enterprise
And dangerous success of bloody wars,
As I intend more good to you and yours
Than ever you or yours by me were harmed!
Queen Elizabeth. What good is covered with the face of heaven,
To be discovered, that can do me good?

King Richard. Th'advancement of your children, gentle lady.
Queen Elizabeth. Up to some scaffold, there to lose their heads?
King Richard. Unto the dignity and height of fortune,
The high imperial type of this earth's glory.
Queen Elizabeth. Flatter my sorrow with report of it;
Tell me what state, what dignity, what honour,
Canst thou demise to any child of mine?
King Richard. Even all I have; ay, and myself and all,
Will I withal endow a child of thine;
So in the Lethe of thy angry soul
Thou drown the sad remembrance of those wrongs
Which thou supposest I have done to thee.
Queen Elizabeth. Be brief, lest that the process of thy kindness
Last longer telling than thy kindness' date.
King Richard. Then know, that from my soul I love thy daughter.
Queen Elizabeth. My daughter's mother thinks it with her soul.
King Richard. What do you think?
Queen Elizabeth. That thou dost love my daughter from thy soul:
So from thy soul's love didst thou love her brothers;
And from my heart's love I do thank thee for it.
King Richard. Be not so hasty to confound my meaning:
I mean that with my soul I love thy daughter,
And do intend to make her Queen of England.
Queen Elizabeth. Well then, who dost thou mean shall be her king?

King Richard. Even he that makes her queen: who else should be?
Queen Elizabeth. What, thou?
King Richard. Even so: how think you of it?
Queen Elizabeth. How canst thou woo her?
King Richard. That would I learn of you,
As one being best acquainted with her humour.
Queen Elizabeth. And wilt thou learn of me?
King Richard. With all my heart.
Queen Elizabeth. Send to her, by the man that slew her brothers,
A pair of bleeding hearts; thereon engrave
'Edward' and 'York'; then haply will she weep:
Therefore present to her—as sometimes Margaret
Did to thy father, steeped in Rutland's blood—
A handkerchief; which, say to her, did drain
The purple sap from her sweet brother's body,
And bid her wipe her weeping eyes withal.
If this inducement move her not to love,
Send her a letter of thy noble deeds;
Tell her thou mad'st away her uncle Clarence,
Her uncle Rivers; ay—and for her sake—
Mad'st quick conveyance with her good aunt Anne.
King Richard. You mock me, madam; this is not the way
To win your daughter.
Queen Elizabeth. There is no other way;
Unless thou couldst put on some other shape,
And not be Richard that hath done all this.
King Richard. Say that I did all this for love of her.
Queen Elizabeth. Nay, then indeed she cannot choose but hate thee,
Having bought love with such a bloody spoil.

King Richard. Look what is done cannot be now amended:
Men shall deal unadvisedly sometimes,
Which after-hours gives leisure to repent.
If I did take the kingdom from your sons,
To make amends I'll give it to your daughter.
If I have killed the issue of your womb,
To quicken your increase I will beget
Mine issue of your blood upon your daughter:
A grandam's name is little less in love
Than is the doting title of a mother;
They are as children but one step below,
Even of your mettle, of your very blood;
Of all one pain, save for a night of groans
Endured of her, for whom you bid like sorrow.
Your children were vexation to your youth,
But mine shall be a comfort to your age.
The loss you have is but a son being king,
And by that loss your daughter is made queen.
I cannot make you what amends I would,
Therefore accept such kindness as I can.
Dorset your son, that with a fearful soul
Leads discontented steps in foreign soil,
This fair alliance quickly shall call home
To high promotions and great dignity:
The king, that calls your beauteous daughter wife,
Familiarly shall call thy Dorset brother;
Again shall you be mother to a king,
And all the ruins of distressful times
Repaired with double riches of content.
What! we have many goodly days to see:
The liquid drops of tears that you have shed
Shall come again, transformed to orient pearl,
Advantaging their loan with interest

Of ten times double gain of happiness.
Go, then, my mother, to thy daughter go;
Make bold her bashful years with your experience;
Prepare her ears to hear a wooer's tale;
Put in her tender heart th'aspiring flame
Of golden sovereignty; acquaint the princess
With the sweet silent hours of marriage joys:
And when this arm of mine hath chastiséd
The petty rebel, dull-brained Buckingham,
Bound with triumphant garlands will I come
And lead thy daughter to a conqueror's bed;
To whom I will retail my conquest won,
And she shall be sole victoress, Caesar's Caesar.

Queen Elizabeth. What were I best to say? her father's brother
Would be her lord? or shall I say her uncle?
Or he that slew her brothers and her uncles?
Under what title shall I woo for thee,
That God, the law, my honour, and her love,
Can make seem pleasing to her tender years?

King Richard. Infer fair England's peace by this alliance.

Queen Elizabeth. Which she shall purchase with still-lasting war.

King Richard. Tell her the king, that may command, entreats.

Queen Elizabeth. That at her hands which the king's King forbids.

King Richard. Say she shall be a high and mighty queen.

Queen Elizabeth. To vail the title, as her mother doth.

King Richard. Say I will love her everlastingly.

Queen Elizabeth. But how long shall that title 'ever' last?

King Richard. Sweetly in force unto her fair life's end.
Queen Elizabeth. But how long fairly shall her sweet life last?
King Richard. As long as heaven and nature lengthens it.
Queen Elizabeth. As long as hell and Richard likes of it.
King Richard. Say, I, her sovereign, am her subject love.
Queen Elizabeth. But she, your subject, loathes such sovereignty.
King Richard. Be eloquent in my behalf to her.
Queen Elizabeth. An honest tale speeds best being plainly told.
King Richard. Then plainly to her tell my loving tale.
Queen Elizabeth. Plain and not honest is too harsh a style.
King Richard. Your reasons are too shallow and too quick.
Queen Elizabeth. O no, my reasons are too deep and dead;
Too deep and dead, poor infants, in their graves.
King Richard. Harp not on that string, madam; that is past.
Queen Elizabeth. Harp on it still shall I till heart-strings break.
King Richard. Now, by my George, my garter, and my crown—
Queen Elizabeth. Profaned, dishonoured, and the third usurped.
King Richard. I swear—
Queen Elizabeth. By nothing; for this is no oath:

Thy George, profaned, hath lost his lordly honour;
Thy garter, blemished, pawned his knightly virtue;
Thy crown, usurped, disgraced his kingly glory.
If something thou wouldst swear to be believed,
Swear then by something that thou hast not wronged.
King Richard. Then, by my self—
Queen Elizabeth. Thy self is self-misused.
King Richard. Now, by the world—
Queen Elizabeth. 'Tis full of thy foul wrongs.
King Richard. My father's death—
Queen Elizabeth. Thy life hath it dishonoured.
King Richard. Why then, by God—
Queen Elizabeth. God's wrong is most of all.
If thou didst fear to break an oath with Him,
The unity the king my husband made
Thou hadst not broken, nor my brothers died:
If thou hadst feared to break an oath by Him,
Th'imperial metal, circling now thy head,
Had graced the tender temples of my child,
And both the princes had been breathing here,
Which now, two tender bedfellows for dust,
Thy broken faith hath made the prey for worms.
What canst thou swear by now?
King Richard. The time to come.
Queen Elizabeth. That thou hast wrongèd in the time o'erpast;
For I myself have many tears to wash
Hereafter time, for time past wronged by thee.
The children live whose fathers thou hast slaughtered,
Ungoverned youth, to wail it in their age;
The parents live whose children thou hast butchered,
Old barren plants, to wail it with their age.
Swear not by time to come; for that thou hast
Misused ere used, by times ill-used o'erpast.

King Richard. As I intend to prosper and repent,
So thrive I in my dangerous affairs
Of hostile arms! myself myself confound!
Heaven and fortune bar me happy hours!
Day, yield me not thy light; nor, night, thy rest!
Be opposite, all planets of good luck,
To my proceeding!—if, with dear heart's love,
Immaculate devotion, holy thoughts,
I tender not thy beauteous princely daughter!
In her consists my happiness and thine;
Without her, follows to myself and thee,
Herself, the land, and many a Christian soul,
Death, desolation, ruin, and decay:
It cannot be avoided but by this;
It will not be avoided but by this.
Therefore, dear mother—I must call you so—
Be the attorney of my love to her;
Plead what I will be, not what I have been—
Not my deserts, but what I will deserve;
Urge the necessity and state of times,
And be not peevish-fond in great designs.
Queen Elizabeth. Shall I be tempted of the devil thus?
King Richard. Ay, if the devil tempt you to do good.
Queen Elizabeth. Shall I forget myself to be myself?
King Richard. Ay, if yourself's remembrance wrong yourself.
Queen Elizabeth. Yet thou didst kill my children.
King Richard. But in your daughter's womb I bury them:
Where in that nest of spicery they will breed
Selves of themselves, to your recomforture.
Queen Elizabeth. Shall I go win my daughter to thy will?
King Richard. And be a happy mother by the deed.

Queen Elizabeth. I go. Write to me very shortly,
And you shall understand from me her mind.
King Richard. Bear her my true love's kiss [*kissing her*]; and so, farewell. [*she goes*
Relenting fool, and shallow-changing woman!

'*Enter* RATCLIFFE'; CATESBY *following*

How now! what news?
Ratcliffe. Most mighty sovereign, on the western coast
Rideth a puissant navy; to our shores
Throng many doubtful hollow-hearted friends,
Unarmed, and unresolved to beat them back:
'Tis thought that Richmond is their admiral;
And there they hull, expecting but the aid
Of Buckingham to welcome them ashore.
King Richard. Some light-foot friend post to the Duke of Norfolk:
Ratcliffe, thyself—or Catesby; where is he?
Catesby. Here, my good lord.
King Richard. Catesby, fly to the duke.
Catesby. I will, my lord, with all convenient haste.
King Richard. Ratcliffe, come hither! post to Salisbury:
When thou comest thither—[*to Catesby*] Dull unmindful villain,
Why stay'st thou here, and go'st not to the duke?
Catesby. First, mighty liege, tell me your highness' pleasure,
What from your grace I shall deliver to him.
King Richard. O, true, good Catesby: bid him levy straight
The greatest strength and power that he can make,
And meet me suddenly at Salisbury.

Catesby. I go. [*he goes*

Ratcliffe. What may it please you, shall I do at Salisbury?

King Richard. Why, what wouldst thou do there before I go?

Ratcliffe. Your highness told me I should post before.

King Richard. My mind is changed.

'*Enter* LORD STANLEY'

Stanley, what news with you?

Stanley. None good, my liege, to please you with the hearing;
Nor none so bad, but well may be reported.

King Richard. Hoyday, a riddle! neither good nor bad!
What need'st thou run so many miles about,
When thou mayest tell thy tale the nearest way?
Once more, what news?

Stanley. Richmond is on the seas.

King Richard. There let him sink, and be the seas on him!
White-livered runagate, what doth he there?

Stanley. I know not, mighty sovereign, but by guess.

King Richard. Well, as you guess?

Stanley. Stirred up by Dorset, Buckingham, and Morton,
He makes for England, here to claim the crown.

King Richard. Is the chair empty? is the sword unswayed?
Is the king dead? the empire unpossessed?
What heir of York is there alive but we?
And who is England's king but great York's heir?
Then, tell me, what makes he upon the seas?

Stanley. Unless for that, my liege, I cannot guess.
King Richard. Unless for that he comes to be your liege,
You cannot guess wherefore the Welshman comes.
Thou wilt revolt and fly to him, I fear.
Stanley. No, my good lord; therefore mistrust me not.
King Richard. Where is thy power then to beat him back?
Where be thy tenants and thy followers?
Are they not now upon the western shore,
Safe-conducting the rebels from their ships?
Stanley. No, my good lord, my friends are in the north.
King Richard. Cold friends to me: what do they in the north,
When they should serve their sovereign in the west?
Stanley. They have not been commanded, mighty king:
Pleaseth your majesty to give me leave,
I'll muster up my friends, and meet your grace
Where and what time your majesty shall please.
King Richard. Ay, ay, thou wouldst be gone to join with Richmond:
But I'll not trust thee.
Stanley. Most mighty sovereign,
You have no cause to hold my friendship doubtful:
I never was nor never will be false.
King Richard. Go then, and muster men; but, leave behind
Your son, George Stanley: look your heart be firm,
Or else his head's assurance is but frail.
Stanley. So deal with him as I prove true to you.
[*goes*

'Enter a Messenger'

Messenger. My gracious sovereign, now in Devonshire,
As I by friends am well advértiséd,
Sir Edward Courtney, and the haughty prelate,
Bishop of Exeter, his elder brother,
With many moe confederates, are in arms.

'Enter another Messenger'

2 *Messenger.* In Kent, my liege, the Guildfords are in arms;
And every hour more competitors
Flock to the rebels and their power grows strong.

'Enter another Messenger'

3 *Messenger.* My lord, the army of great Buckingham—
King Richard. Out on you, owls! nothing but songs of death? [*he strikes him*
There, take thou that, till thou bring better news.
3 *Messenger.* The news I have to tell your majesty
Is that, by sudden floods and fall of waters,
Buckingham's army is dispersed and scattered;
And he himself wand'red away alone,
No man knows whither.
King Richard. I cry thee mercy:
There is my purse to cure that blow of thine.
Hath any well-advisèd friend proclaimed
Reward to him that brings the traitor in?
3 *Messenger.* Such proclamation hath been made, my lord.

'Enter another Messenger'

4 *Messenger.* Sir Thomas Lovel and Lord Marquis Dorset,

'Tis said, my liege, in Yorkshire are in arms.
But this good comfort bring I to your highness,
The Breton navy is dispersed by tempest:
Richmond, in Dorsetshire, sent out a boat
Unto the shore, to ask those on the banks
If they were his assistants, yea or no;
Who answered him, they came from Buckingham
Upon his party: he, mistrusting them,
Hoised sail and made his course again for Brittany.
King Richard. March on, march on, since we are up in arms;
If not to fight with foreign enemies,
Yet to beat down these rebels here at home.

CATESBY returns

Catesby. My liege, the Duke of Buckingham is taken;
That is the best news: that the Earl of Richmond
Is with a mighty power landed at Milford
Is colder tidings, yet they must be told.
King Richard. Away towards Salisbury! While we reason here,
A royal battle might be won and lost:
Some one take order Buckingham be brought
To Salisbury; the rest march on with me.
[*a flourish as they go*

[4. 5.] *LORD STANLEY's house*

LORD STANLEY and SIR CHRISTOPHER URSWICK, a priest

Stanley. Sir Christopher, tell Richmond this from me:
That in the sty of the most deadly boar
My son George Stanley is franked up in hold:
If I revolt, off goes young George's head;
The fear of that holds off my present aid.
So, get thee gone; commend me to thy lord.
Withal say that the queen hath heartily consented
He should espouse Elizabeth her daughter.
But, tell me, where is princely Richmond now?
Christopher. At Pembroke, or at Ha'rford-west, in Wales.
Stanley. What men of name resort to him?
Christopher. Sir Walter Herbert, a renownéd soldier;
Sir Gilbert Talbot, Sir William Stanley,
Oxford, redoubted Pembroke, Sir James Blunt,
And Rice ap Thomas, with a valiant crew,
And many other of great name and worth:
And towards London do they bend their power,
If by the way they be not fought withal.
Stanley. Well, hie thee to thy lord; I kiss his hand:
My letter will resolve him of my mind.
Farewell. [*they go*

[5. 1.] *Salisbury. An open place*

Enter a Sheriff 'with halberds', leading BUCKINGHAM *'to execution'*

Buckingham. Will not King Richard let me speak with him?

Sheriff. No, my good lord; therefore be patient.

Buckingham. Hastings, and Edward's children, Grey and Rivers,
Holy King Henry, and thy fair son Edward,
Vaughan, and all that have miscarriéd
By underhand corrupted foul injustice,
If that your moody discontented souls
Do through the clouds behold this present hour,
Even for revenge mock my destruction!
This is All-Souls' day, fellow, is it not?

Sheriff. It is, my lord.

Buckingham. Why, then All-Souls' day is my body's doomsday.
This is the day which in King Edward's time
I wished might fall on me when I was found
False to his children and his wife's allies;
This is the day wherein I wished to fall
By the false faith of him whom most I trusted;
This, this All-Souls' day to my fearful soul
Is the determined respite of my wrongs:
That high All-Seer which I dallied with
Hath turned my feignéd prayer on my head,
And given in earnest what I begged in jest.
Thus doth He force the swords of wicked men
To turn their own points in their masters' bosoms:
Thus Margaret's curse falls heavy on my neck;
'When he,' quoth she, 'shall split thy heart with sorrow,

Remember Margaret was a prophetess.'
Come, lead me, officers, to the block of shame;
Wrong hath but wrong, and blame the due of blame.
[*they pass on*

[5. 2.] *The camp near Tamworth*

'*Enter* RICHMOND, OXFORD, BLUNT, HERBERT, *and others, with drum and colours*'

Richmond. Fellows in arms, and my most loving friends,
Bruised underneath the yoke of tyranny,
Thus far into the bowels of the land
Have we marched on without impediment;
And here receive we from our father Stanley
Lines of fair comfort and encouragement.
The wretched, bloody, and usurping boar,
That spoils your summer fields and fruitful vines,
Swills your warm blood like wash, and makes his trough
In your embowelled bosoms—this foul swine
Is now even in the centre of this isle,
Near to the town of Leicester, as we learn.
From Tamworth thither is but one day's march.
In God's name, cheerly on, courageous friends,
To reap the harvest of perpetual peace
By this one bloody trial of sharp war.
Oxford. Every man's conscience is a thousand men,
To fight against this guilty homicide.
Herbert. I doubt not but his friends will turn to us.
Blunt. He hath no friends but what are friends for fear,
Which in his dearest need will fly from him.

Richmond. All for our vantage. Then, in God's name, march:
True hope is swift, and flies with swallow's wings;
Kings it makes gods, and meaner creatures kings.
[*they march away*

[5. 3.] *Bosworth Field*

'*Enter* KING RICHARD *in arms with* NORFOLK', *the* EARL OF SURREY, *and others*

King Richard. Here pitch our tent, even here in Bosworth field.
My Lord of Surrey, why look you so sad?
Surrey. My heart is ten times lighter than my looks.
King Richard. My Lord of Norfolk,—
Norfolk. Here, most gracious liege.
King Richard. Norfolk, we must have knocks, ha? must we not?
Norfolk. We must both give and take, my loving lord.
King Richard. Up with my tent! Here will I lie to-night—
But where to-morrow? Well, all's one for that.
Who hath descried the number of the traitors?
Norfolk. Six or seven thousand is their utmost power.
King Richard. Why, our battalia trebles that account:
Besides, the king's name is a tower of strength,
Which they upon the adverse faction want.
Up with the tent! Come, noble gentlemen,
Let us survey the vantage of the ground.
Call for some men of sound direction:

Let's lack no discipline, make no delay;
For, lords, to-morrow is a busy day.
[*they depart to survey the ground the while soldiers pitch the royal tent*

Enter, on the other side of the field, RICHMOND, SIR WILLIAM BRANDON, OXFORD, *and others. Soldiers pitch Richmond's tent*

Richmond. The weary sun hath made a golden set,
And by the bright tract of his fiery car
Gives token of a goodly day to-morrow.
Sir William Brandon, you shall bear my standard.
Give me some ink and paper in my tent:
I'll draw the form and model of our battle,
Limit each leader to his several charge,
And part in just proportion our small power.
My Lord of Oxford, you, Sir William Brandon,
And you, Sir Walter Herbert, stay with me.
The Earl of Pembroke keeps his regiment:
Good Captain Blunt, bear my good-night to him,
And by the second hour in the morning
Desire the earl to see me in my tent:
Yet one thing more, good captain, do for me—
Where is Lord Stanley quartered, do you know?
Blunt. Unless I have mista'en his colours much,
Which well I am assured I have not done,
His regiment lies half a mile at least
South from the mighty power of the king.
Richmond. If without peril it be possible,
Sweet Blunt, make some good means to speak with him,
And give him from me this most needful note.
Blunt. Upon my life, my lord, I'll undertake it;
And so, God give you quiet rest to-night!

Richmond. Good night, good Captain Blunt.
Come, gentlemen,
Let us consult upon to-morrow's business:
In to my tent! the dew is raw and cold.
['*they withdraw into the tent*'

Enter, to his tent, KING RICHARD, NORFOLK, RATCLIFFE, CATESBY, *and others*

King Richard. What is't o'clock?
Catesby. It's supper-time, my lord;
It's nine o'clock.
King Richard. I will not sup to-night.
Give me some ink and paper.
What, is my beaver easier than it was?
And all my armour laid into my tent?
Catesby. It is, my liege; and all things are in readiness.
King Richard. Good Norfolk, hie thee to thy charge;
Use careful watch, choose trusty sentinels.
Norfolk. I go, my lord.
King Richard. Stir with the lark to-morrow, gentle Norfolk.
Norfolk. I warrant you, my lord. [*he goes*
King Richard. Catesby!
Catesby. My lord?
King Richard. Send out a pursuivant-at-arms
To Stanley's regiment; bid him bring his power
Before sunrising, lest his son George fall
Into the blind cave of eternal night. [*Catesby goes*
Fill me a bowl of wine. Give me a watch.
Saddle white Surrey for the field to-morrow.
Look that my staves be sound, and not too heavy.
Ratcliffe!
Ratcliffe. My lord?

King Richard. Saw'st thou the melancholy Lord Northumberland?
Ratcliffe. Thomas the Earl of Surrey and himself,
Much about cock-shut time, from troop to troop
Went through the army, cheering up the soldiers.
King Richard. So, I am satisfied. A bowl of wine:
I have not that alacrity of spirit
Nor cheer of mind that I was wont to have.
Set it down. Is ink and paper ready?
Ratcliffe. It is, my lord.
King Richard. Bid my guard watch. Leave me.
Ratcliffe, about the mid of night come to my tent
And help to arm me. Leave me, I say.
[*Ratcliffe goes; Richard withdraws into his tent*

Enter STANLEY '*to* RICHMOND *in his tent*', *Lords and others attending*

Stanley. Fortune and victory sit on thy helm!
Richmond. All comfort that the dark night can afford
Be to thy person, noble father-in-law!
Tell me, how fares our loving mother?
Stanley. I, by attorney, bless thee from thy mother,
Who prays continually for Richmond's good:
So much for that. The silent hours steal on,
And flaky darkness breaks within the east.
In brief, for so the season bids us be,
Prepare thy battle early in the morning,
And put thy fortune to th'arbitrement
Of bloody strokes and mortal-staring war.
I, as I may—that which I would I cannot—
With best advantage will deceive the time,
And aid thee in this doubtful shock of arms:

But on thy side I may not be too forward,
Lest, being seen, thy brother, tender George,
Be executed in his father's sight.
Farewell: the leisure and the fearful time
Cuts off the ceremonious vows of love
And ample interchange of sweet discourse
Which so long sund'red friends should dwell upon.
God give us leisure for these rites of love!
Once more, adieu: be valiant, and speed well!

Richmond. Good lords, conduct him to his regiment:
I'll strive with troubled thoughts to take a nap,
Lest leaden slumber peise me down to-morrow,
When I should mount with wings of victory:
Once more, good night, kind lords and gentlemen.
[*they leave: Richmond kneels*
O Thou, whose captain I account myself,
Look on my forces with a gracious eye;
Put in their hands thy bruising irons of wrath,
That they may crush down with a heavy fall
Th'usurping helmets of our adversaries!
Make us thy ministers of chastisement,
That we may praise thee in the victory!
To thee I do commend my watchful soul,
Ere I let fall the windows of mine eyes:
Sleeping and waking, O, defend me still!
['*sleeps*'

'*The Ghost of* PRINCE EDWARD, *son to Henry the Sixth*', *appears between the tents*

Ghost. ['*to Richard*'] Let me sit heavy on thy soul to-morrow!
Think how thou stab'st me in my prime of youth
At Tewkesbury: despair therefore, and die!

['*to Richmond*'] Be cheerful, Richmond; for the wrongéd souls
Of butchered princes fight in thy behalf:
King Henry's issue, Richmond, comforts thee.
[*vanishes*

'*The Ghost of* HENRY THE SIXTH' *appears*

Ghost. [*to Richard*] When I was mortal, my anointed body
By thee was punchéd full of deadly holes:
Think on the Tower and me: despair, and die!
Harry the Sixth bids thee despair and die!
['*to Richmond*'] Virtuous and holy, be thou conqueror!
Harry, that prophesied thou shouldst be king,
Doth comfort thee in thy sleep: live and flourish!
[*vanishes*

'*The Ghost of* CLARENCE' *appears*

Ghost. [*to Richard*] Let me sit heavy on thy soul to-morrow!
I that was washed to death with fulsome wine,
Poor Clarence, by thy guile betrayed to death.
To-morrow in the battle think on me,
And fall thy edgeless sword: despair, and die!
['*to Richmond*'] Thou offspring of the house of Lancaster,
The wrongéd heirs of York do pray for thee:
Good angels guard thy battle! live, and flourish!
[*vanishes*

'*The Ghosts of* RIVERS, GREY, *and* VAUGHAN' *appear*

Ghost of Rivers. [*to Richard*] Let me sit heavy on thy soul to-morrow,
Rivers, that died at Pomfret! Despair, and die!

Ghost of Grey. [*to Richard*] Think upon Grey, and let thy soul despair!
Ghost of Vaughan. [*to Richard*] Think upon Vaughan, and, with guilty fear,
Let fall thy lance: despair, and die!
'*All to Richmond*' Awake, and think our wrongs in Richard's bosom
Will conquer him! awake, and win the day!
[*they vanish*

'*The Ghost of* LORD HASTINGS' *appears*

Ghost. [*to Richard*] Bloody and guilty, guiltily awake,
And in a bloody battle end thy days!
Think on Lord Hastings: despair, and die!
['*to Richmond*'] Quiet untroubled soul, awake, awake!
Arm, fight, and conquer, for fair England's sake!
[*vanishes*

'*The Ghosts of the two young Princes*' *appear*

Ghosts. [*to Richard*] Dream on thy cousins smotheréd in the Tower:
Let us be lead within thy bosom, Richard,
And weigh thee down to ruin, shame, and death!
Thy nephews' souls bid thee despair and die!
['*to Richmond*'] Sleep, Richmond, sleep in peace, and wake in joy;
Good angels guard thee from the boar's annoy!
Live, and beget a happy race of kings!
Edward's unhappy sons do bid thee flourish.
[*they vanish*

'*The Ghost of* ANNE *his wife*' *appears*

Ghost. ['*to Richard*'] Richard, thy wife, that wretched Anne thy wife,

That never slept a quiet hour with thee,
Now fills thy sleep with perturbations:
To-morrow in the battle think on me,
And fall thy edgeless sword: despair, and die!
['*to Richmond*'] Thou quiet soul, sleep thou a quiet sleep:
Dream of success and happy victory!
Thy adversary's wife doth pray for thee. [*vanishes*

'*The Ghost of* BUCKINGHAM' *appears*

Ghost. ['*to Richard*'] The first was I that helped thee to the crown;
The last was I that felt thy tyranny:
O, in the battle think on Buckingham,
And die in terror of thy guiltiness!
Dream on, dream on, of bloody deeds and death:
Fainting, despair; despairing, yield thy breath!
['*to Richmond*'] I died for hope ere I could lend thee aid:
But cheer thy heart, and be thou not dismayed:
God and good angels fight on Richmond's side;
And Richard falls in height of all his pride. [*vanishes*

King '*Richard starts out of his dream*'

King Richard. Give me another horse! bind up my wounds!
Have mercy, Jesu!—Soft, I did but dream.
O coward conscience, how dost thou afflict me!
The lights burn blue. It is now dead midnight.
Cold fearful drops stand on my trembling flesh.
What do I fear? myself? there's none else by.
Richard loves Richard; that is, I am I.
Is there a murderer here? No—yes, I am:
Then fly. What, from myself? Great reason why—
Lest I revenge. Myself upon myself?

Alack, I love myself. For any good
That I myself have done unto myself?
O, no! Alas, I rather hate myself
For hateful deeds committed by myself!
I am a villain: yet I lie, I am not.
Fool, of thyself speak well: fool, do not flatter.
My conscience hath a thousand several tongues,
And every tongue brings in a several tale,
And every tale condemns me for a villain.
Perjury, perjury, in the high'st degree;
Murder, stern murder, in the dir'st degree;
All several sins, all used in each degree,
Throng to the bar, crying all 'Guilty! guilty!'.
I shall despair. There is no creature loves me;
And if I die, no soul will pity me:
Nay, wherefore should they, since that I myself
Find in myself no pity to myself?
Methought the souls of all that I had murdered
Came to my tent, and every one did threat
To-morrow's vengeance on the head of Richard.

RATCLIFFE comes to the tent

Ratcliffe. My lord!
King Richard. Zounds! who is there?
Ratcliffe. My lord; 'tis I. The early village cock
Hath twice done salutation to the morn;
Your friends are up, and buckle on their armour.
King Richard. O Ratcliffe, I have dreamed a fearful dream!
What thinkest thou, will all our friends prove true?
Ratcliffe. No doubt, my lord.
King Richard. Ratcliffe, I fear, I fear—
Ratcliffe. Nay, good my lord, be not afraid of shadows.

King Richard. By the apostle Paul, shadows to-night
Have struck more terror to the soul of Richard
Than can the substance of ten thousand soldiers
Arméd in proof, and led by shallow Richmond.
'Tis not yet near day. Come, go with me;
Under our tents I'll play the eaves-dropper,
To hear if any mean to shrink from me. [*they go*

'Enter the Lords to RICHMOND, *sitting in his tent'*

Lords. Good morrow, Richmond!
Richmond. Cry mercy, lords and watchful gentlemen,
That you have ta'en a tardy sluggard here!
Lords. How have you slept, my lord?
Richmond. The sweetest sleep and fairest-boding dreams
That ever ent'red in a drowsy head
Have I since your departure had, my lords.
Methought their souls whose bodies Richard murdered
Came to my tent and cried on victory:
I promise you my soul is very jocund
In the remembrance of so fair a dream.
How far into the morning is it, lords?
Lords. Upon the stroke of four.
Richmond. Why, then 'tis time to arm and give direction.

'His oration to his soldiers', who gather about the tent

More than I have said, loving countrymen,
The leisure and enforcement of the time
Forbids to dwell upon: yet remember this,
God and our good cause fight upon our side;
The prayers of holy saints and wrongéd souls,
Like high-reared bulwarks, stand before our faces.
Richard except, those whom we fight against

Had rather have us win than him they follow:
For what is he they follow? truly, gentlemen,
A bloody tyrant and a homicide;
One raised in blood, and one in blood established;
One that made means to come by what he hath,
And slaughtered those that were the means to help him;
A base foul stone, made precious by the foil
Of England's chair, where he is falsely set;
One that hath ever been God's enemy.
Then, if you fight against God's enemy,
God will in justice ward you as his soldiers;
If you do sweat to put a tyrant down,
You sleep in peace, the tyrant being slain;
If you do fight against your country's foes,
Your country's fat shall pay your pains the hire;
If you do fight in safeguard of your wives,
Your wives shall welcome home the conquerors;
If you do free your children from the sword,
Your children's children quits it in your age.
Then, in the name of God and all these rights,
Advance your standards, draw your willing swords.
For me, the ransom of my bold attempt
Shall be this cold corpse on the earth's cold face;
But if I thrive, the gain of my attempt
The least of you shall share his part thereof.
Sound drums and trumpets bold and cheerfully;
God and Saint George! Richmond and victory!
[*they march away*

KING RICHARD returns with RATCLIFFE

King Richard. What said Northumberland as touching Richmond?
Ratcliffe. That he was never trainéd up in arms.

King Richard. He said the truth: and what said Surrey then?
Ratcliffe. He smiled and said 'The better for our purpose.'
King Richard. He was in the right; and so indeed it is. ['*clock strikes*'
Tell the clock there. Give me a calendar.
Who saw the sun to-day?
Ratcliffe. Not I, my lord.
King Richard. Then he disdains to shine; for by the book
He should have braved the east an hour ago:
A black day will it be to somebody.
Ratcliffe!
Ratcliffe. My lord?
King Richard. The sun will not be seen to-day;
The sky doth frown and lour upon our army.
I would these dewy tears were from the ground.
Not shine to-day! Why, what is that to me
More than to Richmond? for the selfsame heaven
That frowns on me looks sadly upon him.

NORFOLK enters in haste

Norfolk. Arm, arm, my lord; the foe vaunts in the field.
King Richard. Come, bustle, bustle. Caparison my horse.
Call up Lord Stanley, bid him bring his power:
I will lead forth my soldiers to the plain,
And thus my battle shall be orderéd:
My foreward shall be drawn out all in length,
Consisting equally of horse and foot;
Our archers shall be placéd in the midst:
John Duke of Norfolk, Thomas Earl of Surrey,
Shall have the leading of this foot and horse.

They thus directed, we will follow
In the main battle, whose puissance on either side
Shall be well wingéd with our chiefest horse.
This, and Saint George to boot! What think'st
thou, Norfolk?

Norfolk. A good direction, warlike sovereign.
This found I on my tent this morning.

[*he shows him a paper*

King Richard. [*reads*] 'Jockey of Norfolk, be not
too bold,
For Dickon thy master is bought and sold.'
A thing deviséd by the enemy.
Go, gentlemen, every man unto his charge:
Let not our babbling dreams affright our souls:
Conscience is but a word that cowards use,
Devised at first to keep the strong in awe:
Our strong arms be our conscience, swords our law.
March on, join bravely, let us to it pell-mell;
If not to heaven, then hand in hand to hell.

'*His oration to his army*'

What shall I say more than I have inferred?
Remember whom you are to cope withal—
A sort of vagabonds, rascals, and runaways,
A scum of Bretons, and base lackey peasants,
Whom their o'er-cloyéd country vomits forth
To desperate ventures and assured destruction.
You sleeping safe, they bring to you unrest;
You having lands, and blest with beauteous wives,
They would distrain the one, distain the other.
And who doth lead them but a paltry fellow,
Long kept in Bretagne at our mother's cost?
A milksop, one that never in his life
Felt so much cold as over shoes in snow?

Let's whip these stragglers o'er the seas again,
Lash hence these overweening rags of France,
These famished beggars, weary of their lives,
Who, but for dreaming on this fond exploit,
For want of means, poor rats, had hanged themselves.
If we be conquered, let men conquer us,
And not these bastard Bretons, whom our fathers
Have in their own land beaten, bobbed, and thumped,
And in record left them the heirs of shame.
Shall these enjoy our lands? lie with our wives?
Ravish our daughters? ['*drum afar off*'] Hark! I hear their drum.
Fight, gentlemen of England! fight, bold yeomen!
Draw, archers, draw your arrows to the head!
Spur your proud horses hard, and ride in blood
Amaze the welkin with your broken staves!

'*Enter a Messenger*'

What says Lord Stanley? will he bring his power?
Messenger. My lord, he doth deny to come.
King Richard. Off with his son George's head!
Norfolk. My lord, the enemy is past the marsh:
After the battle let George Stanley die.
King Richard. A thousand hearts are great within my bosom:
Advance our standards, set upon our foes;
Our ancient word of courage, fair Saint George,
Inspire us with the spleen of fiery dragons!
Upon them! Victory sits on our helms. [*they charge*

[5. 4.] '*Alarum: excursions*'. *Re-enter* NORFOLK; *and forces fighting; to him* CATESBY

Catesby. Rescue, my Lord of Norfolk, rescue, rescue!
The king enacts more wonders than a man,

Daring and opposite to every danger:
His horse is slain, and all on foot he fights,
Seeking for Richmond in the throat of death.
Rescue, fair lord, or else the day is lost!

'Alarums. Enter RICHARD'

King Richard. A horse! a horse! my kingdom for a horse!
Catesby. Withdraw, my lord; I'll help you to a horse.
King Richard. Slave, I have set my life upon a cast,
And I will stand the hazard of the die.
I think there be six Richmonds in the field;
Five have I slain to-day instead of him.
A horse! a horse! my kingdom for a horse!
[*they pass on*

[5. 5.] *'Alarum. Enter RICHARD with RICHMOND; they fight; RICHARD is slain'*

A retreat is sounded; then with a flourish re-enter RICHMOND, and STANLEY 'bearing the crown, with divers other lords'

Richmond. God and your arms be praised, victorious friends!
The day is ours; the bloody dog is dead.
Stanley. Courageous Richmond, well hast thou acquit thee.
Lo, here, this long usurpéd royalty
From the dead temples of this bloody wretch
Have I plucked off, to grace thy brows withal:
Wear it, enjoy it, and make much of it.
Richmond. Great God of heaven, say Amen to all!
But, tell me, is thy young George Stanley living?
Stanley. He is, my lord and safe in Leicester town;
Whither, if it please you, we may now withdraw us.

Richmond. What men of name are slain on either side?
Stanley. John Duke of Norfolk, Walter Lord Ferrers,
Sir Robert Brakenbury, and Sir William Brandon.
Richmond. Inter their bodies as becomes their births:
Proclaim a pardon to the soldiers fled
That in submission will return to us:
And then, as we have ta'en the sacrament,
We will unite the white rose and the red.
Smile heaven upon this fair conjunction,
That long have frowned upon their enmity!
What traitor hears me, and says not Amen?
England hath long been mad, and scarred herself;
The brother blindly shed the brother's blood,
The father rashly slaughtered his own son,
The son, compelled, been butcher to the sire:
All that divided York and Lancaster,
Divided in this dire division,
O, now let Richmond and Elizabeth,
The true succeeders of each royal house,
By God's fair ordinance conjoin together!
And let their heirs, God if his will be so,
Enrich the time to come with smooth-faced peace,
With smiling plenty and fair prosperous days!
Abate the edge of traitors, gracious Lord,
That would reduce these bloody days again,
And make poor England weep in streams of blood!
Let them not live to taste this land's increase
That would with treason wound this fair land's peace!
Now civil wounds are stopped, Peace lives again:
That she may long live here, God say Amen! [*they go*

GLOSSARY

Abate (vb.), blunt (O.E.D. 8); 5. 5. 35

Abject (sb.), lit. outcast, hence (quibblingly) most servile of subjects; 1. 1. 106

Abortive, monstrous, like a monster; 1. 2. 21; 1. 3. 228

Abroach, on foot; 1. 3. 325

Abroad (of news) in circulation; 1. 1. 134, 135 (quibblingly); 2. 3. 3

Abuse, (i) do violence to; 1. 3. 52; (ii) bring disgrace or dishonour upon; 3. 7. 199

Account (sb.), (i) estimation; 3. 2. 69; (ii) computation, reckoning; 5. 3. 11

Account (vb.), reckon on, expect; 3. 2. 70.

Acquittance (vb.), acquit (v. note); 3. 7. 233

Adulterate, adulterous (cf. *Lucr.* 1645); 4. 4. 69

Advance, raise; 1. 2. 40; 5. 3. 264, 348.

Advantage (sb.), chance, opportunity; 3. 5. 73; 4. 1. 49; 5. 3. 92

Advantage (vb.), 'add to the value of' (O.E.D. 3); 4. 4. 324

Adventure (vb.), risk; 1. 3. 116

Advertise, notify, inform; 4. 4. 500

Advised (to be), 'consider, reflect, act after consideration' (O.E.D.); 1. 3. 318; 4. 4. 516

Aery, brood of young eagles; 1. 3. 264, 270

Affected, disposed; 3. 1. 171

After-supper, O.E.D. glosses 'time between supper and bedtime', but the ex. at *M.N.D.* 5. 1. 34 proves that 'late supper, rere-supper' (Onions) is correct; 4. 3. 31

Aged, characteristic of, or belonging to, old age (cf. *Temp.* 4. 1. 261 'aged cramps'); 4. 4. 16

A-high, on high, aloft (here only in Sh.); 4. 4. 86

Aim (sb.), target, mark; 4. 4. 89

Alarum, signal 'to arms' with drum and trumpet; 1. 1. 7; 4. 4. 152 S.D.; 5. 4., 5. 5. S.D. (head)

Ally, relative (cf. *Rom.* 3. 1. 114; *A.Y.L.* 5. 4. 186); 2. 1. 30

Almost, even (cf. *K. John*, 4. 3. 43). Used to intensify a rhetor. question (O.E.D. 4); 3. 5. 34

Amaze, terrify, alarm (O.E.D. 3, 'Obs.'); 5. 3. 341

Amble, walk with affected gait; 1. 1. 17

Anchor, fix firmly; 4. 4. 232

Answer (vb. abs. and trans.); atone, atone (or pay) for; 1. 3. 194; 4. 2. 90

Apparent, manifest; 2. 2. 130, 136; 3. 5. 30

Arch, pre-eminent (gen. in evil sense); 4. 3. 2

Argue, prove, evince; 3. 7. 40, 174

Aspect, glance, appearance; 1. 2. 154

ASSURANCE, security; 4. 4. 497

ATONEMENT, reconciliation; 1. 3. 36

ATTAINDER, dishonouring stain (O.E.D. 2b); prob. variant of 'attainture' (*2 H. VI*, 1. 2. 106); 3. 5. 32

ATTEND, accompany, wait on; 3. 7. 244; 4. 4. 196

ATTORNEY, (i) advocate, pleader (O.E.D. 4); 4. 4. 127, 414; (ii) deputy, proxy; 5. 3. 83

AVOIDED, Either (i) shunned, or (ii) expelled (cf. *Err.* 4. 3. 63; 4. 4. 46); 4. 4. 219

AWARD (vb.), decree; 2. 1. 14

AWELESS, inspiring no awe; 2. 4. 52

BAR, lit. the wooden rail before a judge's seat; fig. a tribunal (v. O.E.D. 22); 5. 3. 199

BARBED. Of a horse, armed or caparisoned with a 'barb', i.e. 'a protective covering for the breast and flanks...made of metal plates or of leather with metal spikes or bosses' (O.E.D. 'barb' sb.[2]); 1. 1. 10

BASILISK, fabulous reptile, said to kill by its look or breath (cf. *3 H. VI*, 3. 2. 187); 1. 2. 150

BATTALIA, (<It. battaglia) 'large armed force in battle array' (O.E.D. 2); 5. 3. 11

BATTLE, army, or large armed force; 1. 3. 130; 5. 3. 24, 138, 292, 299

BAYNARD'S CASTLE, on the N. bank of the Thames, close to the present Blackfriars Bridge. Had been Ric., Dk. of York's London house, and was now Ric., Dk. of Gloucester's; 3. 5. 97

BEAR HARDLY, resent, bear ill-will for (cf. O.E.D. 'bear' vb. 16; *Caes.* G.); 2. 1. 57

BEAVER, helmet (cf. *1 H. IV*, 4. 1. 104). Prop. the face-guard of the helmet; 5. 3. 50

BEHOLDING, beholden, under obligation, indebted; 2. 1. 130

BELIKE, probably; 1. 1. 49; 1. 3. 65

BEND, aim direct, turn. Orig. of the bow; 1. 2. 95

BENEFIT, bestowal of a right; 3. 7. 196

BETTER (vb.), exaggerate, make out better than it is (a sense not in O.E.D.); 4. 4. 122

BID, endured. Past tense of 'bide'; 4. 4. 305

BITTERLY, 'with acrimony' (Schmidt); 3. 7. 192

BLACK, evil; 1. 2. 34; 3. 7. 231; 4. 4. 71

BLACK-FACED, ominously gloomy (cf. *V.A.* 773 'black-faced night'); 1. 2. 158

BLOOD, (i) anger, passion (cf. *Merch.* 1. 2. 17; *Lear*, 4. 2. 64); 1. 2. 15; 5. 3. 340; (ii) family, kinship; 1. 3. 125; 2. 1. 93; 2. 4. 63; 3. 7. 135

BLOOD-SUCKER, blood-thirsty person; 3. 3. 5

BLUNT, rude (cf. *3 H. VI*, 4. 8. 2) or harsh (cf. *3 H. VI*, 5. 1. 86); 1. 3. 104

BLUNTLY, rudely; 4. 3. 45

BOB, strike with the fist, pommel; 5. 3. 334

BOND, ?legal deed of contract (v. note); 4. 4. 77

BOOT, (i) additional item thrown in, something given into the bargain; 4. 4. 65; (ii) 'to boot' = to our help (cf. *Wint.* 1. 2. 80; O.E.D. 7c 'In appreciatory phrases'); 5. 3. 301

BOTTLED, lit. shaped like a leather bottle, (hence) protuberant, swollen; 1. 3. 242 (v. note); 4. 4. 81

BOUGHT AND SOLD, 'betrayed for a bribe' (O.E.D. 'buy' 11b); 5. 3. 305

BRACE, pair (with a touch of contempt); 3. 7. 74

BRAVE (vb.), (i) challenge, defy; 4. 3. 57; (ii) make splendid (cf. *Shrew*, 4. 3. 125); 5. 3. 279

BREAK, interrupt; 1. 4. 76

BREATHING, living, composed of living beings; 1. 1. 21

BRUISE, crush; 5. 2. 2; 5. 3. 110

BULK, trunk, body. A corruption of 'bouk' (= belly, body); not orig. the same word as 'bulk' (= mass, volume); 1. 4. 40

BUNCH-BACKED, hunch-backed; 1. 3. 246; 4. 4. 81

BURTHENED, burdensome; 4. 4. 111

BUTT-END, fag-end; 2. 2. 110

BUY, obtain; 1. 4. 6; 4. 4. 72

BUZZARD, inferior kind of hawk ('useless for falconry' O.E.D.); 1. 1. 133

BY'R LADY, by Our Lady, i.e. the Virgin Mary; 2. 3. 4

CACODEMON, evil spirit. Actually the Gk. κακοδαίμων = a devil; 1. 3. 144

CAITIFF, pitiful wretch; 4. 4. 101

CAPABLE, gifted; 3. 1. 155

CAPARISON (vb.), cover with a rich horse-covering; 5. 3. 289

CAREFUL, full of care or anxiety; 1. 3. 83

CARNAL, carnivorous (O.E.D. 6; only inst. given). Perh. by mistaken assoc. with 'carnage'; 4. 4. 56

CAUSE, case, affair; 3. 5. 65

CENSURE, judgement, opinion; 2. 2. 144; 3. 5. 67

CEREMONIOUS, scrupulous about forms; 3. 1. 45

CERTIFY, inform with certainty, assure; 3. 2. 10

CHAMBERLAIN, male servant for bed-chambers at an inn; 'Lord C.' = officer in charge of the king's private apartments; 1. 1. 77, 123; 1. 3. 38; 3. 2. 111

CHANCE (vb.), 'how chance?' = how does it come about that?; 4. 2. 97

CHANGE, variation, fickleness; 3. 5. 80

CHARACTER, writing, written record; 3. 1. 81

CHARGE, (i) orders; 1. 1. 105; so 'give in charge' = give orders; 1. 1. 85; (ii) division of troops under a specific officer's command; 5. 3. 25, 307

CHARGES, AT, at the expense (of); 1. 2. 255

CHARM, witch's incantation; 1. 3. 215

CHARTER, 'immunity' granted by royal charter (O.E.D. 3); 3. 1. 54

CHECK, rebuke; 1. 4. 136; 3. 7. 150

CHEERLY, cheerily; 5. 2. 14

CHURCHMAN, clergyman (O.E.D. gives no ex. of the mod. sense before 1677); 3. 7. 48

CIRCUMSTANCE, 'by circumstance' = in detailed statement; 1. 2. 77, 80

CITE UP, call to mind; 1. 4. 14

CLOSE, (i) secret; 1. 1. 158; 4. 2. 34; (ii) shut up, confined; 4. 2. 50

CLOSELY, in secret; 3. 1. 159

CLOSET, private room, bedroom; 2. 1. 134

CLOSURE, enclosure; 3. 3. 10

CLOUDY, gloomy, melancholy; 2. 2. 112

CLOUT, piece of cloth, rag; 1. 3. 177

COCKATRICE, basilisk (q.v.); 4. 1. 55

COCK-SHUT TIME, evening twilight—the time either (*a*) when poultry are shut up, or (*b*) when woodcock 'shoot' through the glades of a wood, and can be caught by nets stretched across the opening (O.E.D. prefers (*a*)); 5. 3. 70

COG, lit. cheat, use fraud, hence wheedle (*Cor.* 3. 2. 133), fawn, use flattery (*M.W.W.* 3. 3. 44); 1. 3. 48

COLD, (i) tepid; 4. 4. 485; (ii) discouraging (O.E.D. 9); 4. 4. 535

COMFORTABLE, cheering, cheerful; 4. 4. 174

COMMENTING, pondering, brooding; 4. 3. 51

COMPETITOR, associate, partner; 4. 4. 505

COMPLAINING, bewailing, lament (cf. *Lucr.* 1839); 4. 1. 88

COMPLAINT, lament; 2. 2. 67

COMPLOT, conspiracy, plot laid by more than one person; 3. 1. 192, 200

CONCEIT, notion; 3. 4. 49

CONCLUDE, (i) decide; 1. 3. 14; 3. 4. 25; (ii) terminate a transaction; 1. 3. 15

CONDITION, (i) proviso, stipulation; 1. 3. 108; (ii) disposition, character (O.E.D. 11); 4. 4. 158

CONDUCT (sb.), escort, guard; 1. 1. 45

CONFIRMED, lit. 'firmly established'. Hence 'age confirmed' = 'the time of life at which early tendencies and character become fixed' (A.H.T.); 4. 4. 172

CONFOUND, (i) ruin, destroy; 4. 4. 400; (ii) defeat, bring to nought; 2. 1. 14

CONJOIN, unite (O.E.D. cites this as intrans.); 5. 5. 31

CONSEQUENCE, sequel; 4. 2. 15; 4. 4. 6

CONSIDERATE, reflective; 4. 2. 30

CONSIST (in), 'reside, inhere' (O.E.D. 6a, cites this); 4. 4. 407

CONSISTORY, council-chamber (generally eccles.), hence, secret fount of wisdom; 2. 2. 151

CONSORTED, associated, leagued; 3. 4. 70; 3. 7. 137

CONTENT (vb.), satisfy. A euphemism for 'pay' (cf. *Oth.* 3. 1. 1); 3. 2. 110

CONTRACT (sb.), betrothal; 3. 7. 5; (pple.), espoused; 3. 7. 179

CONVENIENT, suitable, fitting; 4. 4. 444

CONVERSATION, sexual intimacy (O.E.D. 3, cites this); 3. 5. 31

CONVEYANCE, underhand removal (generally theft); 4. 4. 284

CONVICT, convicted; 1. 4. 187

COSTARD, lit. a kind of apple; slang for 'head'; 1. 4. 154

COUNTED, accounted, esteemed; 4. 1. 47

COUSIN, (i) nephew; 3. 1. 101–17 (*passim*); 4. 4. 222–3; 5. 3. 151; (ii) grandchild; 2. 2. 8; 2. 4. 9; (iii) formal term of address by a sovereign to a fellow-sovereign or kinsman; 2. 2. 152; 3. 1. 137; 3. 4. 22, 35; 3. 5. 1; 3. 7. 227; 4. 2. 1, 17

COVERT'ST, most secret; 3. 5. 33

COZEN, cheat, defraud; 4. 4. 223

CRAZE, crack, break; 4. 4. 17

CREW, band, company (not disparaging); 4. 5. 15

CROSS (adj.), perverse; 3. 1. 126; (adv.), across (cf. *2 H. VI*, 4. 1. 114); 4. 1. 42

CROSS-ROW, alphabet (from cross prefixed to it formerly in primers); 1. 1. 55

CRY MERCY, v. *mercy*; 1. 3. 235, etc.

CRY ON, cry aloud (in joy or terror). Cf. *Ham.* G.; 5. 3. 231

CUNNING, clever; 3. 1. 135

CURRENT. Of coinage or fig. (i) accepted as genuine; 1. 2. 84; 1. 3. 256; 4. 2. 9; (ii) moving freely; 2. 1. 95

CURST, spiteful; 1. 2. 49

DALLY, trifle (O.E.D. 2b, 3; but only with 'with'); 2. 1. 12; 5. 1. 20

DANGER, power to harm, mischief (O.E.D. 1, 6); 2. 3. 27

DARE, challenge to a fight; 5. 4. 3

DARKLY, 'gloomily, frowningly' (O.E.D. 3, cites this); 1. 4. 169

DATE, duration (cf. *Son.* 18. 4); 4. 4. 255

DAUB, lit. plaster; hence, 'cover with specious exterior' (O.E.D. 7); 3. 5. 29

DEAL UPON, 'set to work upon' (O.E.D. 18, cites this); 4. 2. 71

DEAR, dire, grievous; 1. 4. 210; 2. 2. 77–9; 5. 2. 21

DECLENSION, decline; 3. 7. 189

DECLINE, go through from beginning to end (from the grammat. sense; cf. *Troil.* 2. 3. 55); 4. 4. 97

DEEP, (i) profound in craft; 1. 1. 149; 1. 3. 224; 2. 1. 38; (ii) profoundly meant or felt; 1. 4. 69; (iii) profoundly skilled or learned; 3. 5. 5; 3. 7. 75; (iv) grievous, heinous; 2. 2. 28; 4. 2. 69; (v) profoundly important (with quibble on i); 3. 7. 67

DEEP-REVOLVING, deeply reflective; 4. 2. 40

DEFACE, efface; 2. 1. 123

DEFACER, effacer; 4. 4. 51

DEGREE, rank; 3. 7. 143, 188

DELIVER, communicate, report; 3. 4. 16; 4. 4. 449

Demise (vb.) transmit. Legal term (O.E.D. 2; here only Sh.); 4. 4. 248

Denier, small copper coin, $\frac{1}{12}$ of a sou; 1. 2. 251

Denounce, pronounce, declare (O.E.D. 1); 1. 3. 180

Deny, refuse; 3. 1. 35; 5. 3. 343

Descant (vb.) (lit.) sing or play extempore variations upon a musical theme (hence fig.) comment, discourse; 1. 1. 27; (sb.) comment; 3. 7. 49

Desert, 'without desert' = undeservedly, and so (transferred to the obj. of action) without cause; 2. 1. 68

Desperately, 'with utter disregard of the consequences' (O.E.D.; cf. *Tw. Nt.* 5. 1. 63); 1. 4. 271

Despiteful, cruel; 4. 1. 37

Determine, (i) decide (but not yet carrying out); 1. 3. 15; 3. 1. 193; 3. 4. 2; (ii) bring to an end; 5. 1. 19

Devoted, sacred, holy; 1. 2. 35

Devotion, (i) devout occupation; 3. 7. 103; (ii) devout 'purpose, intent' (O.E.D. 7, cites this); 4. 1. 9

Dickon, familiar form of 'Dick', Richard; 5. 3. 305

Diet, mode of life (O.E.D. 1); 1. 1. 139

Diffused, disordered, i.e. shapeless (v. note and cf. *H. V*, 5. 2. 61, 'diffused attire'); 1. 2. 78

Digest, (*a*) modern sense; (*b*) 'settle and arrange methodically' (O.E.D. 3); 3. 1. 200

Dignity, sovereignty, royal power (Schmidt); 3. 7. 196

Direction, (i) capacity for tactics; 5. 3. 16; (ii) 'tactical arrangement' (G.M.); 5. 3. 236, 302

Discipline, (i) milit. training or experience (O.E.D. 3b); 3. 7. 16; (ii) mod. sense; 5. 3. 17

Discover, disclose, reveal; 4. 4. 241

Disgracious, displeasing, out of favour (O.E.D. 2); 3. 7. 112; 4. 4. 178

Dismal, ill-boding, sinister; 1. 4. 7; 3. 3. 12

Dispatch, (i) (abs.) act quickly; 1. 3. 355; 3. 4. 93, 101; (*a*) the same, (*b*) kill; 1. 2. 181; 3. 3. 7; (ii) (trans.) carry out, execute, quickly; 1. 3. 341; 1. 4. 271

Dissemble, 'cloak or disguise [a person or feeling] by a feigned appearance' (O.E.D. 1); 1. 1. 19; 2. 1. 8

Distain, bring dishonour on; 5. 3. 322

Distrain, confiscate (v. note); 5. 3. 322

Divinely, piously; 3. 7. 62

Do, 'do naught', do wickedness (v. *naught*), i.e. copulate (v. O.E.D. 'do' 16b); 1. 1. 98, 99

Doom (sb.), death, destruction (cf. *Lucr.* 672, *Son.* 14. 14); 4. 4. 12

Doom (vb.), decide on, adjudge; 2. 1. 103; 3. 4. 64

Doting, tender, fond; 4. 4. 301

Doubtful, apprehensive; 4. 4. 436

DRAW FORTH, rescue; 3. 7. 198

DULL, gloomy (cf. *2 H. IV*, 4. 3. 95); 1. 3. 196

DUTEOUS, dutiful (cf. *Lucr.* 1360, *Lear*, 4. 6. 258); 3. 5. 64

DUTY, respect, reverence; 1. 3. 253; 2. 2. 108; 3. 3. 3; 'do duty' = make obeisance; 1. 3. 251

EDGE, sword (cf. *Cor.* 5. 6. 113); 5. 5. 35

EFFEMINATE, gentle, tender, as a woman; 3. 7. 211

EGALLY, equally; 3. 7. 213

ELVISH-MARKED, marked by malign fairies at birth; 1. 3. 228

EMBASSAGE, message (O.E.D. 2); 2. 1. 3

EMBOWELLED, disembowelled; 5. 2. 10

EMPERY, absolute dominion; or territory under an absolute ruler; 3. 7. 136

END, fragment, remnant (cf. mod. 'candle-end'); 1. 3. 337

ENFORCEMENT, (i) violation; 3. 7. 8; (ii) compulsion, constraint; 3. 7. 233; 5. 3. 238

ENFRANCHISE, set free; 1. 1. 110

ENGROSS, (i) write in the large formal script appropriate to legal documents; 3. 6. 2; (ii) fatten, make fat; 3. 7. 76

ENTERTAIN, (i) while away, spend agreeably (cf. *Lucr.* 1361; O.E.D. 9b); 1. 1. 29; (ii) maintain in one's service, employ (O.E.D. 5); 1. 2. 256; (ii) receive, take; 1. 3. 4; 1. 4. 132

ENTREAT (vb.), treat (O.E.D. 1); 4. 4. 152

ENVIOUS, malicious, malignant; 1. 3. 26; 1. 4. 37

ENVY, malice; 4. 1. 100

ERRONEOUS, criminal (cf. *3 H. VI*, 2. 5. 90; O.E.D. 2); 1. 4. 195

ESTATE, (i) government, regime; 2. 2. 127; (ii) class or rank of persons; 3. 7. 213

EVEN, smooth, free of obstacles; 3. 7. 157

EVIDENCE, (abs. for concr.), witness; 1. 4. 183

EXCELLENT (adv.), pre-eminently; 4. 4. 52

EXCLAIM (sb.), outcry (cf. *R. II*, 1. 2. 2); 1. 2. 52; 4. 4. 135

EXCURSION, sortie, sally; 5. 4. S.D. (head)

EXERCISE, sermon, act of worship. The term seems to be post-reformation but was used by both Catholics and Protestants; 3. 2. 109; 3. 7. 64

EXHALE, draw forth, cause to flow (O.E.D. vb.[2] 1b); 1. 2. 58, 165

EXPEDIENT, expeditious; 1. 2. 216

EXPEDITION, march; 4. 4. 136

EXPIATE (pple.), fully come (the only inst. in O.E.D.; but cf. *Son.* 22. 4); 3. 3. 23

EXPLOIT, deed (simply); 4. 2. 34

EXPOSTULATE, set forth one's views; 3. 7. 192

EXTREMITY, extreme severity (O.E.D. 6); 1. 1. 65

FACTIOUS, taking sides in a quarrel or strife; 1. 3. 128; 2. 1. 20

FACTOR, agent; 3. 7. 134; 4. 4. 72

FAIR (adj.), (i) happy, prosperous; 4. 4. 352; (ii) handsome; 1. 3. 47

FAIR (adv.), courteously; 4. 4. 152

FAIR BEFALL YOU, good fortune come to you; 1. 3. 282; 3. 5. 46

FAIRLY, (i) beautifully; 3. 6. 2; (ii) happily; 4. 4. 353

FAITHFUL, true-believing; 1. 4. 4

FALCHION, sword; 1. 2. 94

FALL (sb.) (i) lapse into sin; 3. 7. 97; (ii) downward stroke (of a sword) (cf. *Oth.* 2. 3. 234); 5. 3. 111

FALL (vb.), let fall, drop; 1. 2. 182 (S.D.); 1. 3. 353; 5. 3. 135, 163

FALSE-BODING, uttering false prophecies; 1. 3. 247

FALSELY, wrongly, fraudulently. A quibble; 5. 3. 251

FAME, common report, rumour; 1. 4. 83

FAT, choicest produce (O.E.D. 2c); 5. 3. 258

FATHER-IN-LAW, step-father (v. O.E.D.); 1. 4. 49; 5. 3. 81

FAULTLESS, innocent (cf. *2 H. VI*, G. 'faulty'); 1. 3. 178

FEAR (vb.), fear for (the life of); 1. 1. 137; 3. 1. 148 (with obj. understood)

FEATURE, 'good shape, comeliness' of the whole body (O.E.D. 1b); 1. 1. 19

FET, fetched; 2. 2. 121

FIGURE, portray; 1. 2. 193

FIRE-NEW, lit. fresh from the mint; 1. 3. 256

FLATTERER (v. *flattering*); 1. 4. 264

FLATTERING, raising false hopes; 4. 4. 85

FLEETING, 'fickle, inconstant' (O.E.D.); 1. 4. 55

FLESHED. Originally term of venery and falconry, of hounds or hawks excited to the chase by being given flesh to eat; hence, inured to bloodshed; 4. 3. 6

FLOURISH, varnish, embellishment; 1. 3. 241; 4. 4. 82

FLOUT, gibe, taunt; 2. 4. 24

FOIL, setting of a jewel; hence, that which sets off something to advantage; 5. 3. 250

FOND, foolish; 3. 4. 80; 5. 3. 330

FOOT-CLOTH, a richly ornamented covering for a horse, hanging down to the ground on each side; 3. 4. 83

FOR, (i) because; 1. 1. 58; 2. 2. 95; (ii) in expressions denoting the thing staked ('for my life'); 4. 1. 3

FOREWARD, vanguard; 5. 3. 293

FORFEIT, something to which the right is lost by the commission of a crime; here loosely 'remission of the forfeit' (J.); 2. 1. 100

FORM, (i) good order; 3. 1. 200; (ii) established method or procedure; 3. 5. 41; (iii) military formation (cf. *2 H. IV*, 4. 1. 20); 5. 3. 24

Formal, following the usual form, typical (cf. O.E.D. 3); 3. 1. 82

Forward, (i) early; 3. 1. 94; (ii) precocious; 3. 1. 155; (iii) eager, ardent; 3. 2. 46; 5. 3. 94; (iv) prompt; 3. 4. 63

Frank up, shut up in a 'frank' or sty (cf. *2 H. IV*, 2. 2. 145); 1. 3. 314; 4. 5. 3

From, (i) free from; 3. 5. 32; (ii) apart from, at variance with; 4. 4. 259, 260, 261; (iii) away from; 5. 3. 284

Fulsome, excessively satiating or cloying; 5. 3. 132

Gallant-springing ('full of manly promise' Herford); 1. 4. 221

Garland, royal crown (cf. O.E.D. 3a); 3. 2. 40

Gentle, (i) noble in rank; 2. 1. 80; (with iron. quibble on 'gentle' = tender, kind); 1. 3. 163; (ii) as a complimentary epithet; 4. 3. 28

George, jewel on which is a figure of St George, the pendant to the collar which is a part of the insignia of the Garter; 4. 4. 367, 370

Gone, overwhelmed (cf. *R. II*, 2. 1. 184, and 'overgone' *3 H. VI*, 2. 5. 123); 4. 3. 20

Good, (i) 'good time of day', v. *time*; 1. 1. 122; 1. 3. 18; (ii) 'do good (to a person)' = be of use to, bestow benefits upon; 4. 3. 33

Goodly, (*a*) fine, (*b*) favourable; 5. 3. 21

Gossip, intimate friend, crony; 1. 1. 83

Grace (sb.), (i) virtue, sense of duty; 1. 3. 55; 2. 1. 121; (ii) favour; 2. 1. 77; 2. 3. 10; 3. 4. 90, 95; (iii) virtuous property (O.E.D. 13a); 2. 4. 13; (iv) divine grace; 3. 4. 96; 4. 4. 219, 221

Grace (vb.), 'gratify, delight' (O.E.D. 6); 4. 4. 175

Gracious, (i) godly, righteous; 2. 4. 20, 21; 3. 2. 56; 3. 7. 65; 3. 7. 100; (ii) favourable, favouring; 5. 3. 109

Graffed, grafted; 3. 7. 127

Gramercy, 'God reward you' (from Old Fr. 'grant merci' may God reward you greatly); response of superior to inferior's respectful good wish; 3. 2. 105

Grand, principal, chief; 4. 4. 52

Gratulate, greet; 4. 1. 10

Grave, (i) weighty; 2. 3. 20; (ii) worthy, venerable; 3. 7. 227

Green, recently established, not long concluded; 2. 2. 127

Grief, hardship; 3. 1. 114

Gross, stupid; 3. 6. 10

Grossly, stupidly; 4. 1. 80

Grossness, 'coarseness, want of refinement' (O.E.D.), here = 'the vulgar, practical standard' (A.H.T.) of the workaday world (v. note); 3. 1. 46

Ground, plain-song or bass on which a 'descant' (*q.v.*) is sung; 3. 7. 49

Grounded, fixed, rooted, established; 1. 3. 29

Gull, simpleton, dupe; 1. 3. 328

HA? eh?; 1. 3. 234; 5. 3. 5

HALBERD, (i) weapon of the 15th and 16th centuries, 'a kind of combination of spear and battle-axe... mounted on a handle 5 to 7 feet long' (O.E.D.); 1. 2. 40; (ii) halberdier; 1. 2. S.D. (head); 5. 1. S.D. (head)

HAP, fortune; 1. 2. 17; 1. 3. 84

HAPPY, propitious, favourable; 3. 7. 172

HARDLY BORNE (v. *bear hardly*); 2. 1. 57

HARSH, discordant; 4. 4. 361

HATCHES, movable planks forming a kind of deck (O.E.D. 3a); 1. 4. 13, 17.

HAUGHT, haughty; 2. 3. 28

HAUGHTY, aspiring (v. note); 4. 2. 36

HEAP, great company; 2. 1. 54

HEARKEN AFTER, enquire about, seek for (O.E.D. 6); 1. 1. 54

HEAVILY, sorrowfully, sadly; 1. 4. 1; 2. 3. 40

HEAVY, (i) grievous; 1. 4. 14; 3. 1. 5; (ii) sorrowful; 3. 1. 149

HEDGEHOG, term of abuse 'applied to a person who is regardless of others' feelings' (O.E.D.); 1. 2. 102

HERALD, messenger; 1. 1. 72

HEREAFTER (adj.), future (cf. *1 H. VI*, 2. 2. 10); 4. 4. 391

HIGH-REACHING, ambitious; 4. 2. 31

HOISE, hoist; 4. 4. 528

HOLD (sb.), custody, imprisonment; 4. 5. 3

HOLD (vb.), continue, always preserve so; 3. 2. 104

HOLP. Old past tense of 'help'; 1. 2. 107; 4. 4. 45

HOYDAY (obs. form of 'heyday'), exclamation of surprise, impatience etc.; 4. 4. 460

HULL (vb.), drift with furled sail; 4. 4. 439

HUMBLE, gentle, kind (sense not recorded in O.E.D.; but cf. *L.L.L.* 5. 2. 628); 1. 2. 164

HUMILITY, humanity (cf. *Merch.* 3. 1. 64; *L.L.L.* 4. 3. 346). Cf. Huloet, *Abecedarium*, 1552 'Humilitie is a gentlenes of the mynde, or a gentle patience without angre or wrathe' (cited Furness); 2. 1. 74; 3. 7. 17

HUMOUR, (i) mood, inclination; 1. 4. 119; (ii) disposition; 4. 4. 270

HUMPHREY HOUR. Unexplained (v. note); 4. 4. 176

IDEA, image (O.E.D. 7); 3. 7. 13

IDLE, (i) vain, trifling; 1. 1. 31; (ii) useless; 3. 1. 103, 105

ILL-DISPERSING, scattering, or spreading, evil; 4. 1. 53

ILL-FAVOURED, ugly, ill-looking; 3. 5. S.D. (head)

IMAGE, likeness, copy; 2. 1. 124; 2. 2. 50

IMAGINATION, something dreamt of, but not realised in experience; 1. 4. 80

IMPEACHMENT, accusation; 2. 2. 22

IMPERIAL, kingly; 4. 4. 245, 383

IMPORT (vb.), involve, concern; 3. 7. 68

INCAPABLE, unable to understand (cf. *Ham.* 4. 7. 177); 2. 2. 18

INCENSE (vb.), instigate, incite (O.E.D. 4); 1. 3. 85; 3. 1. 152; 3. 2. 29

INCLINATION, disposition; 3. 1. 178

INCLUSIVE, encircling; 4. 1. 59

INCREASE, (i) offspring, progeny; 4. 4. 298; (ii) produce of the soil; 5. 5. 38

INDEX, lit. 'a table of contents prefixed to a book' (O.E.D. 5a), hence, prologue or preface to a book or play; 2. 2. 149; 4. 4. 85

INDIRECT, not open or straightforward; 1. 4. 218; 3. 1. 31

INDIRECTLY, 'not in express terms' (O.E.D. 2b); 4. 4. 226

INDUCTION (lit.) dramatic prologue in dialogue (hence, fig.) 'preparation' (J.), initial step in an undertaking (O.E.D. 3c); 1. 1. 32; 4. 4. 5

INFECTION, plague (O.E.D. 5); 1. 2. 78

INFER, allege, adduce (O.E.D. 2); 3. 5. 74 (v. note); 3. 7. 12, 32; 4. 4. 344; 5. 3. 314

INGENIOUS, 'able, talented' (O.E.D. 1); 3. 1. 155

INHERITOR, possessor; 4. 3. 34

INSINUATE, ingratiate oneself, curry favour (O.E.D. 2b); 1. 3. 53; 1. 4. 148

INSTANCE, cause (O.E.D. 2); 3. 2. 25

INSULTING, scornfully triumphant, contemptuously exulting; 2. 4. 51

INTELLIGENCER, secret agent; 4. 4. 71

INTEND, pretend; 3. 5. 8; 3. 7. 45

INTENT, design, purpose; 1. 1. 149, 158

INTESTATE, dead without heirs; 4. 4. 128

INWARD, familiar, intimate (O.E.D. 3); 3. 4. 8

IRON, sword; 5. 3. 110

IRON-WITTED, 'dull-witted, stupid' (cf. O.E.D. 'iron' adj. 4; *Rom.* 4. 5. 126; Nashe, ii. 261, 29); 4. 2. 28

IWIS, certainly, assuredly; 1. 3. 102

JACK, (i) low common fellow; 1. 3. 53, 72, 73; (ii) figure of a man on a clock, which strikes the bell for the hours (alluding to (i) also); 4. 2. 111

JEALOUS, suspicious; 1. 1. 81, 92; 3. 1. 36

JET, encroach; 2. 4. 51

JOCKEY, familiar form of 'Jack' or 'John'; 5. 3. 304

JOY, (i) (trans.), rejoice at; 2. 4. 59; (ii) (intrans.), experience joy, be glad; 4. 4. 93

JUMP WITH, coincide (orig. =fall together with), agree; 3. 1. 11

JUST, (i) exact; 4. 4. 110; (ii) due, suitable; 5. 3. 26

KEEP, 'keep the stroke' = (*a*) go on striking (cf. O.E.D. 'keep' 3b, citing *Err.* 3. 1. 61; *Tw. Nt.* 2. 3. 75), (*b*) keep time (cf. O.E.D. 'stroke' 10b); 4. 2. 111

KEEPER, gaoler; 1. 4. 66, 73, 161

KEY-COLD, Lit. as cold as a key; prov. = 'cold in (or 'as') death' (cf. Tilley, K23, and *Lucr.* 1774); 1. 2. 5

KIND, affectionate and gentle by nature; 4. 3. 24

KNOT, (i) company, group, here in a bad sense, e.g. gang; 3. 1. 182 (with a poss. quibble on 'knot' (O.E.D. 13) = tumour); 3. 3. 5; (ii) marriage tie; 4. 3. 42

LABOUR, work for, endeavour to bring about; 1. 4. 246

LACKEY (attrib.), camp follower (O.E.D. 2); 5. 3. 317

LAG, late; 2. 1. 91

LAMELY, (*a*) haltingly, (*b*) (imperfectly, defectively, inefficiently' (O.E.D.); cf. *Gent.* 2. 1. 87 'lamely writ'); 1. 1. 22

LATE (adv.), lately; 2. 2. 149; 3. 1. 99

LAY ON, attribute to. Not recorded by Schmidt or Onions; and by O.E.D. (27) only of 'something objectionable'; 1. 3. 97

LAY OPEN, disclose, display; 3. 7. 15

LEADEN, inert; 3. 1. 176; 4. 3. 52; 5. 3. 105

LEADS, flat roof covered with lead (cf. O.E.D. 'lead' sb.[1] 7); 3. 7. 55

LEAGUE, alliance, compact; 1. 3. 281; 2. 1. 2, 29

LEISURE, time at one's disposal; 5. 3. 97, 238

LESSON (vb.), teach, instruct; 1. 4. 240

LET BLOOD, bleed (surgical). A sardonic euphemism for 'kill' (cf. *Caes.* 3. 1. 153); 3. 1. 183

LETHE, river of Hades (v. note); 4. 4. 251

LEVEL (vb.), aim; 4. 4. 203

LEWD, (i) wicked, vile; 1. 3. 61; (ii) lascivious; 3. 7. 72

LIBEL, defamatory pamphlet (O.E.D. 5); 1. 1. 33

LIGHT (adj.), slight, unimportant; 3. 1. 118

LIGHT-FOOT, nimble; 4. 4. 441

LIGHTLY, (i) commonly, often; 3. 1. 94; (ii) slightly; 1. 3. 45

LIMIT (sb.), prescribed time or period (cf. *R. II*, 1. 3. 151); 3. 3. 7; (vb.), appoint (to an office or command; cf. *Macb.* 2. 3. 51); 5. 3. 25

LINEAL, possessed by right of lineal descent; 3. 7. 121

LIST, choose, like; 3. 5. 83

LIVE, 'live well' = prosper materially (cf. well to live', *Merch.* 2. 2. 49); 1. 4. 143

LIVELIHOOD, animation (O.E.D. sb[2]; cf. *All's.* 1. 1. 52); 3. 4. 55 [withdrawn]

LODGE (vb.), harbour (O.E.D. vb. 2c); 2. 1. 65

LOOK, 'look how' = just as; 1. 2. 203; 'look what' = whatever; 1. 3. 114; 4. 4. 292; 'look when' = as soon as; 1. 3. 290; 3. 1. 194 (v. Mark Eccles, *Sh.'s Use of 'Look How'*, etc., J.E.G.P., xlii. 1943, 386–400)

LOOKER-ON, beholder; 4. 1. 31

LOVE-BED, 'bed for the indulgence of lust' (Schmidt; not in O.E.D. Cf. *Tw. Nt.* 2. 5. 48 'day-bed'); 3. 7. 72

Low, humble, mean; 1. 4. 82

Luxury, lasciviousness, lust; 3. 5. 79

Majesty, 'impressive stateliness of demeanour' (O.E.D.), grandeur; 1. 1. 16; 3. 1. 100

Make, (i) do (only used in questions beginning 'what'), 1. 3. 164; 4. 4. 474; (ii) make up, complete; 2. 1. 44; (ii) muster (cf. *Cor.* 5. 1. 37); 4. 4. 451

Make means, contrive; 5. 3. 40, 248

Malapert, impudent; 1. 3. 255

Malmsey, a strong, sweet wine (orig. from Monemvasia, later from Spain, etc.); 1. 4. 270

Map, 'detailed representation in epitome.... Very common in the 17th c.' (O.E.D. 2); 2. 4. 54

Mark (vb.), brand, set a mark on (cf. 1. 3. 293); 2. 2. 39; 3. 4. 71

Meaning, action intended, purpose; 1. 4. 95; 3. 5. 54

Measure, stately dance; 1. 1. 8

Meed, reward; 1. 4. 228, 282

Mercury, the messenger of the gods in Lat. mythol., shod with winged sandals; 2. 1. 89; 4. 3. 55

Methoughts. Past of the impers. 'methinks'. This 'curious form', not found before Sh., 'prob. owes its "s." to the analogy of *methinks*' (O.E.D.); 1. 4. 9 (v. note), 24, 58

Mettle, substance, stuff (cf. *Macb.* 1. 7. 73); 4. 4. 303

Mew, mew up, coop, shut up. Lit. to put a hawk in a 'mew' (=cage); 1. 1. 38, 132; 1. 3. 139

Minister, servant, agent. Often in Sh. 'angel (good or bad)'; 1. 3. 294; 1. 4. 220; 5. 3. 113

Miscarry, perish, die; 1. 3. 16; 5. 1. 5

Misconster, misjudge (the usu. Sh. form of 'misconstrue'); 3. 5. 60

Misdoubt, have misgivings about; 3. 2. 86

Mistake, misunderstand, take wrongly; 1. 3. 62

Mistrust, anticipate the occurrence of danger or misfortune (cf. *Wint.* 2. 1. 48); 2. 3. 42

Mockery, illusion, unreal appearance (cf. *Macb.* 3. 4. 107); 3. 2. 27

Model, plan; 5. 3. 24

Moe, more; 4. 4. 200, 503

Moiety, small portion, part; 2. 2. 60

Monument, memorial; 1. 1. 6

Moralize, interpret or explain the moral or symbolical meaning (e.g. of a passage in Scripture); hence here 'draw out the hidden meaning of' (Onions); 3. 1. 83

Mortal-staring, glaring fatally, with death in its eyes; 5. 3. 90

Move, exasperate; 1. 3. 248, 249

Much, ''tis much' = it's a serious matter (cf. O.E.D. 'much' 2g); 3. 7. 93

Muse, wonder; 1. 3. 305
Mutual, common ('Now regarded as incorrect' O.E.D.); 2. 2. 113

Namely, particularly (O.E.D. 1); 1. 3. 329
Nature, of, by nature; 1. 3. 230
Naught, wickedness (cf. *do*); 1. 1. 98, 99
Near (adv.), intimately, closely; 1. 1. 112
Need (sb.), (i) distress, straits; 1. 3. 77; (ii) 'for a need' =if necessary, 'at a pinch' (O.E.D. 14c); 3. 5. 84
Need (vb.), be without (some necessary quality); 3. 7. 166
Needful, urgent (cf. *Meas.* 1. 1. 56); 5. 3. 41
Neglect, cause something to be neglected (O.E.D. 5); 3. 4. 24
Neighbour, 'the neighbour to' =privy to; 4. 2. 42
New-appearing, lately become visible (cf. *Son.* 7. 3); 4. 4. 10
Nice, over-subtle (cf. *3 H. VI*, 4. 7. 58; *Shrew*, 3. 1. 80); 3. 7. 175
Niece, granddaughter; 4. 1. 1
Noble, gold coin worth 6*s.* 8*d.*; 1. 3. 82
Nomination, specification (cf. *Merch.* 1. 3. 146); 3. 4. 5

Object (vb.), 'object to' =urge against (O.E.D. 4); 2. 4. 17
Obsequiously, as a dutiful mourner; 1. 2. 3
Occasion, (i) opportunity; 2. 2. 148; (ii) ground, cause; 3. 1. 26
Odds, 'at odds' =at variance; 2. 1. 71
O'er-cloyed, 'filled beyond satiety' (Schmidt); 5. 3. 318
O'erlook, inspect; 3. 5. 17
O'erworn, the worse for wear; hence (of a woman) faded; 1. 1. 81
Offend, (i) harm, wrong, sin against; 1. 4. 177, 178, 219; (ii) annoy; 4. 4. 179
Offer at, menace; 1. 2. 178 S.D.
Office, 'the proper action of an organ or faculty', bodily or mental (O.E.D. 3b; cf. *Oth.* 3. 4. 113); 3. 5. 10
Omit, disregard (O.E.D. 2c); 3. 5. 30
Open, (i) patent; 3. 5. 30; (ii) unobstructed (cf. O.E.D. 19); 4. 2. 73
Opposite (adj.), (i) antagonistic, adverse (astrol.); 2. 2. 94; 4. 4. 216, 403; (ii) ready to face (danger); 5. 4. 3
Order, 'take order' =make arrangements (O.E.D. 14); 3. 5. 105; 4. 2. 50; 4. 4. 538
Orient (adj.), specially lustrous or shining. Orig. of pearl from the Indian seas; then of any pearl (cf. O.E.D. 2b); 4. 4. 323
Outrage, violent conduct or language; 1. 3. 277; 2. 4. 64
Overblown, past; 2. 4. 61
Overgo, exceed; 2. 2. 61
Owe, own (earliest sense); 4. 4. 142

Pack, conspiring gang (cf. *Err.* 4. 4. 101; *Tw. Nt.* 5. 1. 377); 3. 3. 4

Pack-horse, horse of burden; hence, fig. drudge; 1. 3. 122

Pageant, lit. a scene upon a stage or the stage itself; fig. 'a mere empty or specious show' (O.E.D.). The mod. sense of 'a brilliant or stately spectacle' not found until the 19th c.; 4. 4. 85

Pain, labour, effort (physical and mental); 1. 3. 117; 4. 4. 304

Painted, 'unreal, pretended' (O.E.D.); 1. 3. 241; 4. 4. 83

Parcelled, particular, individual; 2. 2. 81

Parlous. Colloq. A contracted form of 'perilous'; 'parlous boy' = enfant terrible (G.M.); 2. 4. 35; 3. 1. 154

Part (vb.), depart; 2. 1. 5

Partly, slightly; 4. 2. 40

Party, side, cause, interest; 3. 2. 47; 4. 4. 191, 527

Passing, surpassingly; 1. 1. 94

Passionate, compassionate (O.E.D. 5b); 1. 4. 119

Pattern, sample, instance; 1. 2. 54

Paul's, St Paul's Cathedral; 1. 2. 30

Pawn, (i) pledge (fig.); 4. 2. 86; (ii) forfeit in exchange for something of less permanent value (cf. *Ant.* 1. 4. 32); 4. 4. 371

Peevish, (i) silly (O.E.D. 1); 1. 3. 194; 4. 2. 94; (ii) perverse (O.E.D. 4); 3. 1. 31

Peevish-fond, perversely foolish; 4. 4. 418

Peise, weigh; 5. 3. 105

Pell-mell, 'with vehement onset' (O.E.D. 3); 5. 3. 312

Perfection, fullness (cf. 'perfectness' *2 H. IV*, 4. 4. 74); 4. 4. 66

Period, conclusion, termination; 'make the period' = round off; 1. 3. 238; 2. 1. 44

Pew-fellow, associate; lit. one who shares the same pew; 4. 4. 58

Pill, rob; 1. 3. 159

Piping, (*a*) characterised by music of peaceful pastoral pipes instead of fifes and drums (O.E.D. 1 b); (*b*) like 'the weak shrill voices of women and children contrasted with the martial voice of men' (Herford); 1. 1. 24

Pirate, any kind of thief 'who robs with violence' (O.E.D. 3); 1. 3. 158

Pitch, lit. height to which falcon soars before swooping down on its prey; here fig., highest point; 3. 7. 188

Plain, guileless, honest (O.E.D. 11); 1. 1. 118; 3. 5. 25

Plant, establish (cf. *Macb.* G.); 2. 2. 100

Pleasing, pleasure; 1. 1. 13

Pluck on, induce (cf. *Meas.* 2. 4. 147; *Tw. Nt.* 5. 1. 366; *K. John*, 3. 1. 57); 4. 2. 62

Point, article, item, piece (cf. O.E.D., A 5; *1 H. IV*, 5. 1. 122 ''tis a point of friendship'); 1. 4. 99

Politic, sagacious (in political affairs) 2. 3. 20

Post (sb.), extreme speed; 3. 5. 72

Post (vb.), take post-horses (*q.v.*); hence, go with speed; 2. 2. 142; 3. 2. 17; 4. 4. 441, 445

Post-horse. To travel 'post' was to make use of relays of horses stationed at stages along the highway of c. 10 miles; 1. 1. 146

Power, armed force; 4. 4. 451, 480, 534; 5. 3. 38, 290

Precedent, 'original from which a copy is made' O.E.D. (Cf. *K. John*, 5. 2. 3); 3. 6. 7

Preposterous, contrary to nature; 2. 4. 63

Presence, (i) assembly, company; 1. 3. 54; (ii) the royal presence-chamber and those within it; 2. 1. 58, 79, 85

Presentation, (*a*) semblance (O.E.D. 5b); (*b*) theatrical representation; 4. 4. 84

Presently, immediately; 3. 1. 34; 3. 2. 16; 4. 2. 26.

Prevent, (i) lit. go before, anticipate; 3. 5. 54; (ii) forestall; 2. 2. 131; 2. 3. 26; 3. 4. 80

Prime, first; 4. 3. 19

Prize, booty; 'make prize of' (here fig.) = capture; 3. 7. 187

Process, story; 4. 3. 32; 4. 4. 254

Prodigious, abnormal, like a monster; 1. 2. 22

Prolong, postpone (cf. *Ado*, 4. 1. 253); 3. 4. 45

Proof, (i) experience; 2. 3. 43; (ii) impenetrable armour; 5. 3. 219

Proper, handsome; 1. 2. 254

Propose, set before one as an object to be attained (O.E.D. 2c); 1. 2. 169

Proudly, haughtily, arrogantly; 4. 3. 42

Provided, well-equipped; 3. 1. 132

Provoke, (i) call forth, give rise to (v. O.E.D. 6); 1. 2. 61; (ii) incite (not only to anger) (O.E.D. 4); 1. 2. 97, 99, 180; 1. 3. 64; 1. 4. 225; 2. 2. 21

Puissance, power, strength; 5. 3. 299

Puissant, strong, mighty; 4. 4. 435

Purchase (sb.), spoil, capture, booty; 3. 7. 187

Purchase (vb.), obtain, gain; 4. 4. 345

Pursuivant. Either (i) junior officer attendant on a herald; or (ii) officer with power to execute warrants and make arrests (v. *1 H. VI*, G.); 3. 2. 93 S.D.; 3. 4. 87

Pursuivant-at-arms = *pursuivant* (i); 5. 3. 59

Put off, set aside, cast off; 3. 7. 183

Quest, jury; 1. 4. 184

Quick, (i) alive; 1. 2. 65; (ii) lively, animated; 1. 3. 5, 196; (iii) (*a*) hasty, (*b*) alive; 4. 4. 362

Quicken, (i) stimulate; 4. 4. 124; (ii) give life to; 4. 4. 298

QUIT, (i) pay (a penalty) for; 4. 4. 20, 64; (ii) requite, reward, 5. 3. 262

RAG. Contemptuous term for a person (O.E.D. 3b); 1. 3. 233; 5. 3. 328

RAGGED, rugged, rough, uneven; 4. 1. 102

RANKLE, cause festering wound, 'breed corruption' (A.W.) (cf. *R. II*, 1. 3. 302); 1. 3, 291

RANSOM, penalty, expiation; 5. 3. 264

RASH-LEVIED, hastily raised; 4. 3. 50

RASHLY, precipitately; 3. 5. 42

RAZE OFF, pull or pluck off; 3. 2. 11; 3. 4. 81

REASON (vb.), (i) question, discuss (O.E.D. 4a); 1. 4. 94; (ii) talk, converse (O.E.D. 2); 1. 4. 160; 2. 3. 39; 3. 1. 132; 4. 4. 536

RECOMFORTURE, consolation (only inst. in O.E.D.); 4. 4. 426

RECURE, remedy (cf. *V.A.* 465; *Son.* 45. 9); 3. 7. 130

REDEEM, deliver, set free; 2. 1. 4

REDUCE, (i) bring; 2. 2. 68; (ii) bring back (orig. sense); 5. 5. 36

RE-EDIFY, rebuild (again at *Tit.* 1. 1. 351 only in Sh.); 3. 1. 71

REFLECT, shine (cf. *Tit.* 1. 1. 226); 1. 4. 31

REMEMBER, 'be remembered' = recollect; 2. 4. 23

REMORSE, (i) compunction; 1. 4. 109; (ii) pity, compassion (O.E.D. 3); 3. 7. 211

REMORSEFUL, compassionate, pitiful; 1. 2. 155

REPETITION, recital, relation; 1. 3. 165

REPLENISHED, perfect, complete; 4. 3. 18

REQUIRE, demand the return of (cf. Luke xii, 20); 2. 2. 95

REQUIT, repay. A variant of 'requite' (cf. *Cor.* 4. 5. 76 (F.) 'requitted'); 1. 4. 68

RESEMBLANCE, external appearance, features (O.E.D. 2); 3. 7. 11

RESERVE, preserve, keep alive (O.E.D. 7; cf. *Meas.* 5. 1. 463); 4. 4. 72

RESOLVE, (i) answer or inform (a person of something); 4. 2. 26; 4. 5. 20; (ii) free from uncertainty, satisfy the curiosity of; 4. 2. 114

RESOLVED, resolute; 1. 3. 340

RESPECT (sb.), consideration, reflection; 3. 7. 175

RESPECT (vb.), (i) pay heed to, take notice of; 1. 3. 296; (ii) value; 1. 4. 152

RESPITE, date to which something is postponed; 5. 1. 19

RETREAT, signal for retreat; 5. 5. S.D. (head)

REVENUE, possession; 3. 7. 158

REVOLVE, consider; 4. 4. 123

RIGHT, true, exact; 3. 7. 13, 103

RIOTOUS, dissolute (cf. *Tim.* 2. 2. 168; *Lear*, 1. 4. 265); 2. 1. 101

RIPE, ready to be enjoyed (like fruit); 3. 7. 158

ROOD, the cross on which Christ was crucified; 3. 2. 75; 4. 4. 166

ROOT (vb.), dig up with the snout (cf. *Tim.* 5. 1. 168; *V.A.* 636); 1. 3. 228

ROUND (vb.), surround, encircle; 4. 1. 60

ROYAL, 'noble, majestic, generous, munificent' (O.E.D. 9); 1. 2. 244

ROYALTY, emblem of sovereignty; 5. 5. 4

RUDE, violent, unrestrained; 2. 2. 38

RUNAGATE, vagabond (cf. *Cymb.* 1. 6. 137), or perh. fugitive, runaway. Properly 'deserter', a later form of 'renegade'; 4. 4. 465

RUNAWAY = *runagate* (q.v.); 5. 3. 316

SACRAMENT, 'receive (take) the sacrament' lit. = receive Holy Communion as a confirmation of a promise (O.E.D. 1 c); (hence) take a strong oath or pledge to perform something; (hence again) swear, bind oneself; 1. 4. 203; 5. 5. 18

SCAR, wound; 5. 5. 23

SCATHE, harm, injury; 1. 3. 317

SCRIVENER, professional scribe; 3. 6. S.D. (head)

SEASON (sb.), time; 1. 4. 61, 76; 5. 3. 87

SEASON (vb.), add relish to, render agreeable; 3. 7. 149

SENIORY, seniority (only instance in O.E.D.); 4. 4. 36

SENNET, notes on a trumpet at the approach or departure of a procession; 3. 1. 150, S.D.

SET (sb.), setting, sunset; 5. 3. 19

SET DOWN, fix a time for (cf. *R. II*, 4. 1. 319); 3. 4. 42

SET HAND (or 'set secretary'), the style of handwriting used for engrossing documents (v. O.E.D., 'set' pple. a. 5); 3. 6. 2

SEVERAL, different, separate; 3. 2. 76; 3. 7. S.D. (head); 5. 3. 25, 193, 194

SHADOW, (i) departed spirit, 'shade'; 1. 4. 53; 5. 3. 216; (ii) illusion, unreal appearance; 5. 3. 215; (iii) (*a*) semblance, (*b*) player; 4. 4. 83

SHAMEFACED, bashful. Properly 'shamefast'; no connexion with 'face'; 1. 4. 138

SHALLOW-CHANGING, moved by trivialities; 4. 4. 432

SHAPE, theatr. guise (O.E.D. 7, 8); 2. 2. 27

SHOT, marksman (cf. *2 H. IV*, 3. 2. 274); 4. 4. 89

SHOULDER, jostle, 'thrust rudely' (Steev.); 3. 7. 128

SIGN, (*a*) mere appearance, semblance, (*b*) banner; 4. 4. 90

SILKEN, effeminate (cf. *L.L.L.* 5. 2. 406; *K. John*, 5. 1. 70; *H. V*, 2 Prol. 2); 1. 3. 53

SIR = '*dominus*, the academic title of a bachelor of arts' (Nares); hence, a form of address to an ordained clergyman; 3. 2. 108; 4. 5. 1

SIRRAH. Form of address to an inferior; 3. 2. 95

SIT, meet in counsel, take counsel together (cf. *H. V*, 5. 2. 81); 3. 1. 173

SLANDER OF (or 'to'), disgrace (to) (O.E.D. 3); 1. 3. 231; 3. 3. 12

Slave, contemptible wretch; 1. 3. 230

Slightly, carelessly (O.E.D. 2); 3. 7. 19

Slug, sluggard. The orig. sense; slug = kind of snail, not found until 18th c.; 3. 1. 22

Smooth (adv.), mildly, blandly; 3. 4. 48; 3. 5. 29

Smooth (vb.), flatter; 1. 3. 48

Smoothing, flattering; 1. 2. 168

So, good!, very well! 2. 1. 1; 4. 4. 183; 5. 3. 72

Soft!, stay!, stop!; 1. 3. 339; 1. 4. 158; 5. 3. 178

Solace (vb.), take comfort, be happy (O.E.D. 3); 2. 3. 30

Sometimes, sometime, once (cf. *Ham.* 1. 1. 49, *Merch.*, 1. 1. 163); 4. 4. 275

Soon at, towards (of time). (Cf. *Err.* 1. 2. 26; 'soon at five o'clock'; 3. 2. 173 'soon at supper-time'); 4. 3. 31

Soothe, cajole, flatter; 1. 3. 298

Sop, lit. a cake or wafer put into a prepared drink and floating on top; 1. 4. 157

Sort (sb.), set, 'crew'; 5. 3. 316

Sort (vb.), (i) contrive (O.E.D. 14); 2. 2. 148; (ii) dispose, ordain (O.E.D. 1 b); 2. 3. 36

Sour, sullen, gloomy (cf. *V.A.* 449, 655); 1. 4. 46

Speed (vb.) (i) (trans.), assist, make to prosper; 2. 3. 6; (ii) (intrans.), have measure of success, fare; 4. 4. 359

Spent, passing (of time); 3. 2. 88

Spleen. Regarded as the seat of various 'humours', hence here = (i) malice; 2. 4. 64; (ii) fiery temper, fiery impetuosity; 5. 3. 350

Splintered, bound up with splints; 2. 2. 118

Spoil (sb.), havoc, destruction; 4. 4. 291

Spoil (vb.), ravage, destroy; 5. 2. 8

Sportive, amorous, wanton (cf. *Son.* 121. 6); 1. 1. 14

Spurn at, oppose contemptuously (cf. 'kick at'); 1. 4. 198

Spurn upon, trample upon, tread under foot; 1. 2. 42

Staff (pl. 'staves'), shaft of lance (O.E.D. 3 a); 5. 3. 65, 341

Stall, install, enthrone; 1. 3. 206

Stamp, lit. = 'design or... marks stamped by authority on a piece of metal in the process of minting' (O.E.D., 2 b); 1. 3. 256

Stand, remain inactive, delay; 1. 3. 350

Stand on, rest on, depend upon; 4. 2. 59

Stand upon (impers.), be of importance to; 4. 2. 56

Start (of a horse), shy; 3. 4. 84

State, high dignity; here, royal position; 1. 3. 112; 3. 2. 83; 3. 7. 205

Stay, support, prevent from falling; 1. 4. 19; 3. 7. 97

Steeled, strengthened; 1. 1. 148

Still (adj.), continual, constant; 4. 4. 230

Still (adv.), continually, always; 1. 3. 222, 278, etc.

Stout, brave; 1. 3. 340

STRAGGLER, rover, vagabond; 5. 3. 327

STRAITLY, strictly; 1. 1. 85

STROKE, cf. *keep*; 4. 2. 111

STRUCK, stricken, advanced; 1. 1. 92

SUBTLE, crafty; 1. 1. 37; 3. 1. 152

SUCCEEDER, heir; 4. 4. 128

SUCCESS, result (good or bad); 4. 4. 237

SUCCESSIVELY, by right of succession; 3. 7. 135

SUDDEN, prompt, quick; 1. 3. 346; 3. 4. 43

SUDDENLY, without delay, promptly, quickly; 4. 2. 19, 20; 4. 4. 452

SUGGESTION, instigation; 3. 2. 100

SURE (adj.), secure, safe; 3. 2. 83

SURFEIT, excessive indulgence (O.E.D. 3); 1. 3. 197

SUSPECT (sb.), suspicion (O.E.D. 1); 1. 3. 89; 3. 5. 32

SWEET (sb.), scented flower (cf. *Ham.* 5. 1. 237); 4. 4. 10

SWELLING, swollen with anger; 2. 1. 52

TA'EN TARDY, v. *tardy*; 4. 1. 52

TAKE ORDER, v. *order*; 3. 5. 105, etc.

TALL, brave; 1. 4. 152

TARDY, 'ta'en tardy' = taken unawares, by surprise; 4. 1. 52

TEEN, grief, sorrow; 4. 1. 97

TEMPER (vb.), fashion, mould (fig. from 'tempering' steel, copper, wax etc.; cf. *Gent.* 3. 2. 64; *Tit.* 4. 4. 110); 1. 1. 65

TENDER (vb.), have tender regard for, be concerned for; 1. 1. 44; 2. 4. 72; 4. 4. 406

TETCHY, fretful, peevish; 4. 4. 169

THIN, thinly covered (cf. *M.N.D.* 2. 1. 109; *R. II*, 3. 2. 112; and *Dial. Dict.* 'thin' 2). Sense not given in O.E.D.; 2. 1. 118

TIME, TIMES, the present time, people at large (cf. *Macb.* 1. 5. 62–3; 5. 8. 55); 4. 4. 417; 5. 3. 92; 'in good, happy, time' = at the right moment, at a happy juncture; 2. 1. 45; 3. 1. 95; 3. 4. 21; 4. 1. 12

TIMELESS, untimely; 1. 2. 117

TIRE, (*a*) make tired, (*b*) prey upon (cf. Marlowe's *Dido*, 5. 1. 317 'The grief that tires upon thine inward soul'); 4. 4. 189

TOUCH (sb.), touchstone (i.e. a hard basaltic stone of dark colour, upon which the metal to be 'assayed' was rubbed so as to produce coloured streaks, which streaks were then compared with those made by standard 'touch-needles'); 4. 2. 8

TOUCH (vb.), (i) concern; 1. 1. 112; 1. 3. 262; 3. 2. 23; (ii) touch upon, mention; 3. 5. 92; 3. 7. 4; (iii) strike at; 2. 3. 26; 2. 4. 25

TOY, (i) idle fancy, freak of fancy; 1. 1. 60; (ii) trifle, trifling ornament; 3. 1. 114

TRACT, track, course; 5. 3. 20

TRIUMPH, public festivity or rejoicing; 3. 4. 42

TRIUMPHANT, jubilant (O.E.D. 4); 3. 2. 81

TRUE-DISPOSING, justly ordaining; 4. 4. 55

TRUTH, fidelity, loyalty; 3. 2. 91; 3. 3. 3

TYPE, lit. distinguishing mark, badge (O.E.D. 3), fig. title, rank (v. note); 4. 4. 245

TYRANNOUS, cruel, ruthless; 4. 3. 1

TYRANNY, violent and lawless action, violence, 2. 4. 51; 3. 7. 9; 5. 3. 168

UNAVOIDED, unavoidable, inevitable; 4. 1. 56; 4. 4. 218

UNGRACIOUS, graceless, devoid of religious virtue (O.E.D. 1); 2. 1. 128

UNHAPPINESS, prodigious nature (Hardin Craig); 1. 2. 25

UNLOOKED, unexpected (O.E.D. 2); 1. 3. 214

UNMANNERED, unmannerly; 1. 2. 39

UNMERITABLE, devoid of merit; 3. 7. 155

UNPROVIDED, unarmed; 3. 2. 73

UNRESPECTIVE, thoughtless, heedless; 4. 2. 29

UNSCARRED, not wounded, unhurt; 4. 4. 210

UNSWAYED, not wielded; 4. 4. 470

UNTAINTED, not attainted, unaccused (O.E.D. 1; the only inst. given); 3. 6. 9

UNTOUCHED, not touched on, unmentioned; 3. 7. 19

UNVALUED, invaluable; 1. 4. 27

UPPER HAND, 'on the upper hand' = in the place of honour, in precedence of (the persons addressed or understood); 4. 4. 37

URGE, put forward as an argument; 1. 3. 146; 1. 4. 108

USE, 'still use' = habitual experience; 4. 4. 230

VAIL, lit. lower (a sail); hence, doff (a crown etc.) in token of submission (O.E.D. 2); 4. 4. 349

VANTAGE, (i) opportunity; 3. 7. 37; (ii) advantage, benefit; 1. 3. 310; 5. 2. 22; (iii) 'condition favourable to success' (Schmidt); 5. 3. 15

VASSAL, 'base, abject person' (O.E.D. 3), wretch; 1. 4. 195

VAST. Blending the senses 'boundless, immense' and 'waste, desolate' (Onions). Cf. Lat. 'vastus'; 1. 4. 39

VAUNT, exult; 5. 3. 288

VENOM (adj.), venomous, poisonous; 1. 3. 291

VERGE, rim, circlet; 4. 1. 59

VICE, comic character in the old Morality plays; also called 'Iniquity'; 3. 1. 82

VIZOR, mask, disguise; here fig. 'virtuous vizor' = semblance of virtue; 2. 2. 28

VOICE, expression of opinion, vote (O.E.D. 10); 3. 2. 53; 3. 4. 19, 28

WAIT UPON, be in attendance on, accompany; 2. 1. 141; 3. 2. 121

WAITING-VASSAL, serving man; 2. 1. 122

WARN, summon (O.E.D. 7); 1. 3. 39

WARRANT (sb.), guarantee, assurance; 'in w. from' = guaranteed by; 3. 7. 33

WASH (sb.), kitchen water and scraps given to pigs; 5. 2. 9

WASH (vb.), 'overwhelm as with water' (Schmidt; cf. *Oth.* 5. 2. 280); 5. 3. 132

WATCH (v. note); 5. 3. 63

WATCHFUL, wakeful, unsleeping; 3. 7. 77; 5. 3. 115

WATERS, heavy rain; 4. 4. 511

WATERY, controlling the tides (cf. *Ham.* 1. 1. 123–4 'moist star', etc.; *M.N.D.* 2. 1. 103, 'governess of floods'); 2. 2. 69

WEIGH, (i) consider; 3. 1. 46; (ii) estimate the value of (with a quibble); 3. 1. 121

WELKIN, sky; 5. 3. 341

WELL-ADVISED, v. *advised*; 1. 3. 318

WELL-SPOKEN, eloquent, persuasive; 1. 1. 29; 1. 3. 348

WHILE (sb.), present time; 'the while' (in exclamations) ellipt. for 'at the present time'; 3. 6. 10

WHITE-LIVERED, cowardly. The liver was considered the seat of courage; 4. 4. 465

WINDOW, eyelid (fig. use from sense 'shutter', for which v. *Caes.* G.); 5. 3. 116

WIT, cleverness, understanding; 3. 1. 50, 85, 86, 132

WITHAL, (i) (adv.) moreover, in addition; 1. 3. 133, 332; 4. 5. 7; (ii) (prep.) with (emphatic); 3. 7. 57, 197; 4. 4. 250; 4. 5. 18; 5. 3. 315; (iii) (adv.) therewith; 4. 4. 279

WITNESS (vb., trans. and intrans.), bear witness to, testify; 3. 5. 69; 4. 4. 60

WITTY, clever, cunning; 4. 2. 41

WORD, phrase (*sententia*); 3. 1. 83

WORSHIP, honour, dignity; 1. 1. 66

WORSHIPFULLY, respectfully, reverentially; 3. 4. 39

WOT. Pres. ind. of 'to wit' = to know; 2. 3. 18 (3rd pers. sing.); 3. 2. 89 (2nd pers. plur.)

WRACK, destruction (O.E.D. sb.[1] 2); 1. 2. 127

WRETCH, i.e. 'poor dear'. Term of pitiful endearment; 2. 2. 6

WRETCHED, hateful, despicable (cf. *Lucr.* 999); 5. 2. 7

YET, now as always; 1. 4. 216

YEOMAN, freeholder under the rank of a gentleman; 5. 3. 338

ZEALOUS, fervently pious; 3. 7. 94

'ZOUNDS.' Expletive = 'God's wounds'; 3. 7. 219; 5. 3. 208